Tales from the Jayhawks Gridiron

Mark Stallard

Foreword by Bill Whittemore

www.SportsPublishingLLC.com

Director of production: Susan M. Moyer
Acquisitions editor: Bob Snodgrass
Project manager: Jim Henehan
Dust jacket design: Joseph T. Brumleve
Developmental editor: Dean Miller
Copy editor: Cynthia L. McNew
Photo editor: Erin Linden-Levy
Marketing manager: Mike Hagan

ISBN: 1-58261-791-0

Printed in the United States of America

Sports Publishing L.L.C.
www.sportspublishingllc.com

To my nephew Brent,
and his enduring passion for KU football

CONTENTS

FOREWORD

Spending most of my life in Tennessee, I really didn't know much about the Kansas-Missouri sports rivalry. I learned a lot about it my junior year at KU, but it still didn't mean much to me when the football team traveled to Columbia to play the Tigers. As the school year progressed, however, and I saw how people reacted watching Kansas-Missouri basketball games, I knew the rivalry was something special. By the time we reached the Mizzou game my senior year, it was a completely different feeling for me. Coach Fambrough was brought in to talk to the team about the history of the rivalry, and that helped me realize just how important the Missouri game is to KU fans.

Coach Fambrough has a hatred for Missouri. It goes all the way back to when he was a player for KU. I specifically remember his speech when we were going to Missouri my junior year and he told us how he'd love to go there and watch the game, but he didn't want to because he knew he'd get into a fight with Tiger fans. He said he'd probably be put in jail if he went to Missouri. He's really a great motivator. Before the Mizzou game my senior year he told us that when our tailbacks got the ball they were not going to go down, they were not going to be stopped. He presented a picture image of what it was going to be like and how we were going to dominate the game.

It turned out Coach Fambrough was pretty right on.

It was a big week for us leading up to the Mizzou game. We had confidence, and we were playing pretty good ball at the time. Going into it, everybody was fired up and ready to go. It was a great feeling coming out on the field for our warm ups and seeing that there was a huge crowd. I'd never seen Memorial Stadium so full. The game itself was one long, awesome feeling. The Kansas fans were ecstatic from the opening kickoff to the final gun. It was a pretty even contest in the first half, but when we scored to go ahead 21-14 in the fourth quarter, I remember thinking, "Yeah, we got 'em on the ropes." I knew if we scored again, they'd definitely start thinking in the back of their heads that they couldn't come back against our defense. We weren't getting very many big yardage plays ourselves, mostly three or four yards at a time, but that really kills a defense. We had a lot of third-down plays and converted on almost all of them. The team scored three touchdowns in the fourth quarter and won going away, 35-14.

It was an amazing sight when the game ended. The crowd stormed the field, tore down the goalposts and we just kind of stood there in awe. I mean it was a great victory, but for me it was overwhelming to see our fans that excited about Kansas football, to see them that thrilled to be Jayhawks. I was so happy that they were just like Coach Fambrough, that they'd give anything to beat Missouri. I stood off in the background and enjoyed how crazy everyone was. They had a blast celebrating the victory, and that's why you play the game. It's for your own inner enjoyment, but it's great to see how much everybody else gets out of it, too.

I think KU's football program is definitely on the right track. They've still got a long way to go, but following the good year we had in 2003, I think the turnaround is in full swing. And I don't think it will stop until they're on top. Coach Mangino does a great job, he's bringing in great players each year, and that's going to be the key thing. Plus, the overall work ethic exhibited by the players and coaches is fantastic. The young players on the team today are devoted to playing hard and winning, especially since they got a taste of it in 2003. They know what it takes to win now, and hopefully will stay driven and continue to fight for it.

Starting the rebuilding process of the KU football program is something I'm glad I was a part of. To go from a ten-loss season to a bowl game in one year is a tremendous leap, and I'm very pleased I was able to contribute to that success. There are many great stories in the long history of Kansas football, and *Tales From the Jayhawks Gridiron* captures the essence of the program. There have been many, many great players and coaches who have graced the sidelines of Memorial Stadium wearing the Crimson and Blue, and I'll always be proud to say I'm a part of that history and tradition.

—Bill Whittemore
March, 2004

ACKNOWLEDGMENTS

One of the best things about putting this book together was the help I received. When I first began *Tales from the Jayhawks Gridiron*, I knew assistance from several different sources was required, and I can honestly say that without it, there would be no book. A lot of little things needed to be combined before I wrote a single word.

As always, there is the usual group of suspects at Sports Publishing who put up with my questions, comments and opinions about everything from the photos to the layout. To Dean Miller, Erin Linden-Levy, Bob Snodgrass, Joe Bannon Jr., Susan Moyer, Jim Henehan, Cynthia McNew, Joseph Brumleve, and the rest of the excellent staff in Champaign—thanks.

Tracking down and conversing with the many former KU football players and coaches whose stories make up the majority of the text was truly a pleasure. Many, many thanks to Kerwin Bell, Marlin Blakeney, Spencer Bonner, Bert Coan, Nolan Cromwell, Chip Budde, Don Davis, Kelly Donohoe, Bobby Douglas, Max Ediger, Emmett Edwards, Ray Evans, Don Fambrough, John Hadl, Harrison Hill, Chip Hilleary, Charlie Hoag, Mike Hubach, David Jaynes, L.T. Levine, Curtis McClinton, Jack Mitchell, Moran Norris, Mike Norseth, Pepper Rodgers, Otto Schnellbacher, Bobby Skahan, Jason Thoren, and especially Bill Whittemore.

Mason Logan, KU's associate media relations director, and his staff provided invaluable help. Carole Hadl in the football office and Louis Ecord of the Williams' Fund office were extremely helpful in tracking down the former players.

Access to the University of Kansas archives was imperative to my work on the book. As they have in the past, Barry Bunch, Kathy Lafferty and the rest of the staff at the Spencer Research Library made sure I got the stuff I needed, when I needed it.

Many thanks to Cameron May, Brent Mathis, Emily Blessing, Sheryl Mathis and especially Luan Billam—who has endured my needs many times in the past—for their excellent transcription help. Alan Barzee, Patricia Van Becelaere and Rob Crouty helped with photos.

Again, thanks to everyone who had a hand in making this book come to life.

INTRODUCTION

From the "phantom fumble" ending of the 1948 Orange Bowl to the 2003 Tangerine Bowl appearance, excitement—good and bad—has always followed KU on the gridiron. This is a book about that excitement, the Kansas Jayhawks football team, as seen through the eyes of the men who coached and played at KU. Chronicled herein are their best moments on the field, a few of their worst, several funny anecdotes, and a couple of sad ones. The University of Kansas has struggled to maintain a winning program through the years, but there was nothing from the men I interviewed that conveyed they wanted to be anywhere but Mount Oread.

However, there was one constant I heard and felt in the voices of the former KU players interviewed—passion. These guys loved playing football for the University of Kansas. It didn't matter if they were All-Americans such as Bobby Douglas, John Hadl or Curtis McClinton, very good players like Mike Norseth or Moran Norris, or simply strong, contributing members of the team like Marlin Blakeney or Max Ediger. It was the same with the coaches, although everyone was hard pressed to match Don Fambrough's overflowing exuberance and love for KU. Kansas football has remained with all of them, not just as memories of games, their teammates and the university, but as a collective intangible that only someone who was there can feel. This book contains their stories.

The following is one of mine:

For three seasons I was a student trainer for the KU football team, which means I helped tape the players' ankles before practice and games, handed out towels and ice packs, and played water boy during the games. I also got an insider's look at the world of college football, a view very few students—let alone fans—get to see. One of the best things about the student trainer experience was Dean "Deaner" Nesmith, one of KU's grand legends of athletics, who I had the honor and pleasure of working for those three seasons. Deaner played football for the Jayhawks from 1933-35 and was the head trainer from 1938 to 1983. His blood and Jayhawk loyalty ran as blue as Don Fambrough's.

The 1977 football season had not been kind to KU. The Jayhawks lost two close games on the road to UCLA and Miami, and were hammered by Oklahoma, Iowa State and Nebraska in Big Eight Conference play. Going into the finale against Missouri, KU had just two wins: a 14-12 squeaker against Washington State and a 29-21 victory over hapless K-State. The Tigers hadn't had much of a season either, and a win by either team in "The Border War" would erase a lot of the year-long frustration both schools had suffered.

The Jayhawks controlled the game from the outset and led throughout. But in the final seconds of play, Kansas faced a third-and-long situation from their own 4-yard line—they held a precarious 24-20 lead. During a timeout KU's head coach Bud Moore, a strict disciple of Alabama's Bear Bryant, and Brian Bethke, the Jayhawks' quarterback, discussed the situation. I happened to be standing next to Deaner on the sideline during the break, who was standing next to Moore. A look of perplexed anxiety covered the coach's face as Bethke calmly waited for his instructions. After an awkward silence, Deaner leaned toward Moore and quietly said, "Take the safety, Coach." When Bethke took the snap moments later, he backed up quickly and ran out of the end zone.

Kansas won the game, 24-22.

For anyone who has ever felt chills from watching a perfectly thrown pass from David Jaynes, thrilled at Nolan Cromwell's precision of running the wishbone, felt the brutal strength of John Riggins thundering into an opposing linebacker, or marveled at Bill Whittemore's collective quarterbacking talents, this is the book for you. Kansas football hasn't had as many "winning" moments as it should have, but it's had countless great players and an absorbing, colorful history. These tales are part of that legacy—enjoy.

Rock Chalk, baby!

CHAPTER 1

Opening Kickoff

"Attack with fury, defend with double fury."
—Edwin M. Hopkins, KU's first varsity
football coach

Kansas hasn't always been a basketball school.
More than a decade before James Naismith, the
inventor of basketball, came to KU, the school
was caught up in the fervor and excitement of college football. The sport had gained popularity on the east coast
throughout the 1870s, but was a little slow reaching the
midwest. When the game finally hit the KU campus,
sometime around 1880, it was immediately embraced by
the students, and attempts were made to organize a univer-

sity team as early as 1882. A game with Washburn College had actually been scheduled in 1884, but for unknown reasons was never played. Finally, a Jayhawker team was put together in 1890, and following a practice game on October 29, KU took the field against Baker University on November 12 in Baldwin, Kansas. KU lost that inaugural game, 22-9. On November 27, the team traveled to Kansas City and lost again, this time to a group of YMCA club members, 18-10.

It was an indifferent start to the Jayhawk tradition of football, but the 1890 squad still had one more game on its schedule, a rematch with Baker in Lawrence.

First Win?

If you check the KU record book, it shows that the Jayhawks notched their first ever football victory on December 8, 1890, defeating Baker University by a score of 14-12. The game was played on the Massachusetts Street Field. It was a glorious afternoon in the annals of KU, and a large crowd of highly spirited KU students yelled the Rock Chalk chant throughout the contest, and celebrated the historical win afterward with a bonfire. But if you did look it up—in the daily newspaper accounts of the day—you might be surprised to learn that the Jayhawks, in reality, lost the game, 12-10.

Huh?

With Kansas trailing 12-10, Baker had the ball near the KU goal before the final snap of the game, and ran a wedge play to get the ball over the line. The ball was fumbled and recovered by Coleman of KU, who ran the length of the field for the apparent game-winning score. But the Baker players contended that the umpire had called time

Wedged Jayhawker bodies battle against Baker in KU's "first ever football victory." *University of Kansas Archives*

out—at the request of a Peairs, a KU player who had already quit the game and was not eligible to ask for time—before Coleman recovered the ball. The umpire, KU professor William H. Carruth, stood by his decision to stop the action, thereby nullifying Coleman's score and making Baker the "official" winner of the game.

For the Kansas students attending the contest it didn't seem to matter. They claimed the game for KU—as their celebration suggests—and as the record book attests, so did the university.

Bad Sports

The game between KU and Iowa at Kansas City's Exposition ballpark on December 17, 1891, had been a classic battle between two evenly matched teams. The Jayhawks held a 14-12 advantage late in the game when a disputed call by the referee ruined the contest, at least for Kansas. The *Kansas City Star's* account of the game read as follows:

> *The Kansas team was not only defeated, but had not shown the most manly spirit. It had disputed the decision of the referee and left the field while it still had a chance to win, in fact when Captain Kinzie (also KU's coach) called his men off the field, the score was 14 to 12 in favor of the Jayhawkers. It is true the Iowas had the ball within ten feet of the Kansas goal line, but there was still a fighting chance. . .*

Kansas had objected to a quick snap play that allowed Iowa to move the ball close to the goal line. After losing his argument with the officials, Kinzie—much to the disapproval of his team—called the Jayhawks off the field. Iowa then scored an uncontested touchdown on the following play and won the game by all reasonable accounts, 18-14.

Once again, as strange as it might seem, the KU record book lists this game as a win for the Jayhawks by the score of 14-12. Not only were these early Jayhawks bad sports, but also bad historians, for this was a game that KU truly lost.

McCook Field

The Jayhawks played their home games in 1890-91 at the Massachusetts Street Field—it was not a suitable place for football. When the question of a new stadium was raised, the answer came from John James

McCook, a prominent New York lawyer who came to KU as a commencement speaker in 1890. McCook became rather fond of the university and contributed $1,500 dollars for a new athletic field as a way to show his interest in the school. He eventually gave another $1,000 as well.

The location for the new field was "Robinson's Pasture," 12 acres of land northwest of the university. The initial grandstand was built to seat 1,000 spectators, and it was agreed upon almost immediately to name the field after its first benefactor.

The Jayhawks played their first football game at McCook Field on October 27, 1892, against Illinois and won, 26-4. The wooden bleachered field served the Jayhawks well, and KU played all home games at McCook for nearly 30 years.

The Mystery of Rollo Krebbs

Kansas fielded a very powerful team in 1899. Behind the coaching prowess of Fielding "Hurry Up" Yost, the Jayhawks rolled to an undefeated season, finishing with an impressive 10 wins against no defeats. Yost would later gain prestige and fame as the University of Michigan's head coach—'99 was his only season at KU.

Kansas had several stars on the team: Bennie Owen, "Cussin' Tom" Smith, and a giant, phenomenal tackle named Rollo Krebbs. Standing six foot three and weighing 210 pounds, Krebbs's appearance in a KU uniform was brief, mysterious and most probably illegal. Regardless, he was by all accounts one of the most dominating players in all of college football that season.

It wasn't until the Jayhawks' eighth game of the season that Krebbs played. *The University Weekly* (KU student newspaper at the time) reported on December 2 that Krebbs had learned the game in Trinidad, Colorado, and enrolled at KU in the fall of 1899 after his parents moved to Birmingham, Kansas. His late appearance in the lineup was explained away—he was gaining experience.

Krebbs first played against Nebraska, and his smashing line play was one of the main reasons the Jayhawks were victorious, 36-20. KU easily defeated Washburn the following week, 23-0. In the season finale against Missouri in Kansas City, Krebbs destroyed the Tigers' line and actually sent two men off the field on stretchers as Kansas humbled Mizzou, 34-6. A celebration was set to honor Krebbs in Lawrence following the game, but the big tackle was not with the team when it returned. It was soon spread around campus that Krebbs was not the simple country boy he said he was. Apparently Coach Yost, to insure victories against the Cornhuskers and Tigers, had recruited Krebbs as a "ringer." The big lineman was actually 27 years old, had never lived in Trinidad, Colorado, or Birmingham, Kansas, played for five seasons on the University of West Virginia's football team, and had even been a professional for one year.

When he finally returned to Lawrence years later, Krebbs said his early departure from KU was because he came to Kansas to play football, not to acquire an education.

Scandalous Behavior

In the two seasons following the 1899 campaign, more ineligible players were used by KU. At the conclusion of the 1901 season, Professor Carruth—the umpire in the KU's "first win"—brought before the

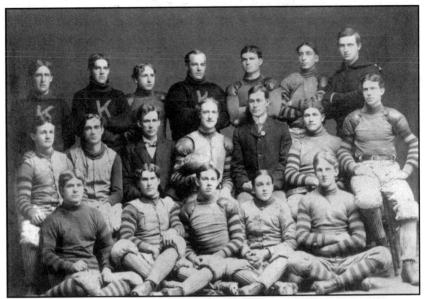

The 1899 Kansas Jayhawks football team posted an impressive 10-0 record. *University of Kansas Archives*

University Council a motion to decrease the game's importance on campus. It failed, and worse, seemed to spawn even more win-at-all-costs efforts by the school to field a powerhouse football squad.

One of the sorriest events in this time period was the firing of Coach Harold S. Weeks by Chancellor Strong. Weeks took over the head coaching duties at KU for the 1903 season and led the Jayhawks to a respectable 6-3 record. But the following spring Weeks was dismissed from his coaching duties by Strong for "allegedly" having sex with a freshman girl.

The K-State Jinx

For the first two decades KU and K-State squared off on the gridiron, the Jayhawks completely dominated their in-state rival. The two schools first met during the 1902 season at McCook Field, and Kansas won easily, 16-0. K-State didn't defeat the Jayhawks until 1906, winning a squeaker in Manhattan, 6-4. From 1907 through the 1923 season, however, Kansas did not lose to the Wildcats (called "Aggies" until 1915). Each successive win brought about another form of the "Jinx," a spell KU seemed to hold over K-State on the football field. Jayhawker fans reveled in their mastery over the Aggies, and each season during this stretch before the start of the game, KU rooters would yell "Jinx! Jinx!" as the K-State team took the field. If Kansas didn't win by three or four touchdowns—which they usually did—a miracle play would occur to either secure a win or tie. Of course it helped that K-State had horrible teams. By 1909, the intense animosity between the two institutions escalated to the point that they did not play one another in 1910.

The Jayhawks finally lost to K-State in 1924, 6-0. That started a string of K-State supremacy in the series that lasted until the end of the 1930s. KU again dominated the rivalry through the late 1960s until the Wildcats broke a 14-game winless streak against the Jayhawks, winning 26-22 in Lawrence. That was also the first season of the modern Governor's Cup Trophy, presented each year to the winner of the game.

The Great Tommy Johnson

Kansas football fans have cheered many great players throughout the program's 114 years of exis-
tence: Gale Sayers, John Riggins, John Hadl, Ray Evans,
Bobby Douglas and David Jaynes, to name a few. As gifted as these players were, there was one player in the early
days of Kansas athletics who not only possessed amazing
athletic gifts, but was also a true inspiration to his teammates, fans and fellow students.

It's been almost 100 years since KU's athletic fields
have felt the physical presence of Tommy Johnson. A
standout in football, basketball and track, Johnson might
very well be the greatest athlete Mount Oread ever had the
privilege of calling her own. He enrolled at KU in the fall
of 1905 and played basketball with another first-year student, Phog Allen. After skipping a year of school, Johnson
returned in '07 to again play basketball, and the following
autumn took over the quarterback position on the football
team. He was an immediate sensation on the gridiron.

The Kansas football team went undefeated in 1908,
posting a 9-0 record to claim the Missouri Valley
Conference championship—Johnson was a major reason
for the team's success. His greatest moment in football
came the following year in Lincoln, Nebraska, when he
returned a punt 70 yards with a wondrous run to score the
game's only touchdown as KU defeated the Cornhuskers,
6-0.

In the 1909 season finale against Missouri, Johnson
was hit so hard that he probably suffered a concussion.
Playing anyway, the star quarterback performed poorly
and the Jayhawks were upset by the Tigers, 12-6, ruining
KU's perfect season and ending their 18-game winning

The Great Tommy Johnson. *University of Kansas Archives*

streak. He was 100 percent for the basketball season, and was so brilliant with his play he became the first Kansas athlete to be named All-America in any sport.

As a child Johnson had suffered from a kidney ailment, and that came back to haunt him and KU at the end of the 1910 football season. The vicious hits he took in the game against Missouri aggravated the kidney problem, and he did not recover. On November 24, 1911, exactly one year after he played his final football game, Tommy Johnson died at Bell Memorial Hospital in Kansas City.

"Tommy Johnson was Kansas' greatest all-around athlete," Phog wrote of his classmate and close friend. "He took advantage of all the time he had. Achievements, not years, must be Time's answer to people seeking reasons why."

His legacy is great and everlasting. Twenty years following his death, his top position in the history of Kansas athletics and the hearts of Jayhawks everywhere was unquestionable, as this testimonial in *1931 Jayhawker Yearbook* shows:

> *There is glory, there is tragedy, in the story of Tommy Johnson, whose name has rightly gone down in university annals as K.U.'s greatest athlete. Many a victorious Jayhawker received the inspiration necessary to come from behind against overwhelming odds from the "Man Who Died for Kansas."*

Rugby Instead of Football?

Football almost died at the University of Kansas in the spring of 1910.

The first ten years of the 20th century had seen college football rise to great heights of popularity across the United States—KU students, faculty and followers held the game very close to their hearts. But the number of brutal injuries, as well as gridiron deaths, had also risen steadily since the game's inception, and several university scholars wanted it off campus (there was only one death from football at KU, in 1896). Once again, Professor Carruth was in the center of a football matter.

". . .scholarship should be exalted to its proper place, and that physical training should not be placed above intellectual culture," Carruth said. Even Chancellor Strong wanted the sport's significant role on campus diminished.

Two of the biggest football opponents were Board of Regents members William Allen White (the School of Journalism at KU is named after him) and J. Willis Gleed. White felt football contributed to the University's materialism, and Gleed thought the sport made "unthinking brutes" of the players. Meanwhile, a movement was started on campus to actually replace football with rugby.

Both movements failed, but at the Missouri Valley Conference meeting in the spring of 1910 (KU was a member of the Valley then), subtle changes were made. The KU-Missouri game, which for 20 years had always been played in Kansas City, was moved to the campuses to get away from the "unsavory" elements of the big city. New rules emphasizing the forward pass were put in place by the National Rules Committee, and some of the fierce brutal play of the game was substantially reduced.

Football survived at Kansas, but the days of the Jayhawkers fielding strong teams and competing for the conference crown year after year were gone.

"Boys, I Had a Dream Last Night"

Nobody loved to tell a tale as much as Phog Allen, KU's great basketball coach. In the fall of 1920, Phog took on the football coaching duties for the university as well, and from his one season on the gridiron sideline experienced many exciting and strange moments. One of the best was his "dream touchdown" story.

Phog was always a big believer in "the hunch"—as he called it—or gut feelings about situations. His intuition helped him many times throughout the course of his great basketball coaching career, and it came in handy a couple of times on the football field. And if he could use his hunches to motivate his players, all the better.

The night before the Iowa State game, so Phog's story goes, he had a dream about his football team flying in an airplane over McCook Field. Of the 11 players' faces he saw in the plane, five were of men who did not normally start. The plane soared over the Iowa State players, then over the goal line at the east end of the field—that was hunch number one. The second part of the dream was more specific.

"I saw Harley Little playing right halfback," Phog wrote in his *Better Basketball* book. "And with the ball tucked under his arm, he started from near our own goal line and I watched him as he crossed Iowa State's goal line, with the ball in his possession."

Phog recounted the dream to his players before the game the next day, inserted the five men from his dream into the starting lineup, instructed them to receive the kickoff and then to run Little around left on the first play of the game. Little got the snap on the first scrimmage following the kickoff, scooted around the left end and raced 85 yards to score what proved to be the only touchdown of the day. Kansas won the game, 7-0.

Phog's hunch, or motivational tactic, worked. He never said whether it was made up or not, and simply mused that, "The game was the thing."

Memorial Stadium

By 1919 it was apparent that McCook Field was no longer an adequate venue for major college football. A Million-Dollar Drive was initiated in the fall of 1920 with the specific purpose of raising the targeted goal of monies to construct a memorial to the KU students who gave their lives in World War I. After careful consideration and debate, it was decided that a stadium and student union building would be built as memorials.

The drive began in earnest on November 18, 1920, less than a week following KU's triumphant, come-from-behind, 20-20 tie with the hated Cornhuskers of Nebraska. After just three days, almost $200,000 was raised. On May 10, 1921, more than 4,000 faculty and students gathered for Stadium Day, and the bleachers at McCook Field were razed. Construction on the new stadium began the following autumn, and two completed sections were used for the game against K-State on October 29.

The formal dedication for Memorial Stadium occurred on November 11, 1922—Armistice Day—and of course the Jayhawks lost to Nebraska. More sections were added to the stadium in 1925, and the north end was closed with a horseshoe in 1927, bringing the capacity to 38,000. In 1963 the west stands were expanded 26 rows to increase capacity to 44,900. When more rows were added to the east side in 1965, the stadium held 51,500.

Several renovations since the mid-sixties have been made to the stadium—new turf, lights, a new concourse, new press box, and video scoreboard. Through the 2003 season, Kansas has played football in Memorial Stadium for 83 years.

The Team with the Uncrossed Goal Line

The Jayhawks had perhaps their finest defensive football team in 1923. Led by Coach "Potsy" Clark, KU shut out six of its eight opponents, and allowed just six points all season—a field goal by Oklahoma and one by Missouri. This great Jayhawks team finished in a tie

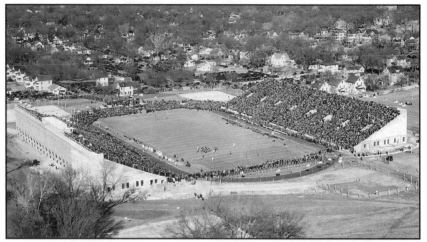

The Jayhawks play to a packed house—Memorial Stadium in 1924. *University of Kansas Archives*

for the Missouri Valley championship, and had an overall record of five wins, no losses and three ties. The annual border war game against Mizzou was played in a Thanksgiving Day blizzard at Memorial Stadium, and the two teams finished in a 3-3 draw.

A side note to the 1923 team: the 83-0 humiliation the Jayhawks laid on Washington (Missouri) that year is still the largest margin of victory in the history of KU football. Only one other time that season did KU score more than nine points.

Kicked Out!

A funny thing happened to the Jayhawks on their way to the Big Six Championship during the 1930 season—they were kicked out of the conference.

The '30 Jayhawks were led by one of the greatest athletes to ever don the crimson and blue, Jim Bausch. A strapping six-foot-two, 200-pound all-around athlete from Wichita, Bausch excelled in football, basketball and track and field. So prolific was his overall athletic ability that he won the decathlon at the 1932 Olympics in Los Angeles. Bausch had originally enrolled at Wichita University (now Wichita State), but transferred to KU when given the opportunity to work for an insurance agency in Topeka. Recruiting at the time was prohibited, and soon there were whispers throughout the conference that Kansas had violated the rules to get Bausch to come to Lawrence.

On the football field KU rolled through its first four opponents, and that's when the other schools in the Big Six began publicly throwing about accusations of illegal recruiting, among other severe violations, specifically naming Bausch. Missouri and Oklahoma yelled the loudest.

Phog Allen, KU's athletic director, and E. H. Lindley, the school's chancellor, protested Kansas's innocence, and refused to declare Bausch ineligible for the remainder of the season. Bausch even issued a public letter stating Mizzou had tried to get him to transfer to Columbia with a lucrative financial deal.

But Missouri wasn't on public trial, KU was. The other five schools in the conference met secretly and collaborated on a plan to oust the Jayhawks—they would refuse to schedule games against KU, which would effectively bar them from the league. When a vote was formally taken to kick KU out of the Big Six, every member school voted to oust the Jayhawks, save K-State. The Wildcats abstained.

Kansas was finally going to declare Bausch ineligible for the remainder of his college career, but when the star athlete decided to play in the East-West Shrine All-Star football game, he effectively forfeited his remaining eligibility. In early December 1930, the conference threw out the earlier vote and KU stayed in the Big Six.

Fighting Irish Stifled

When the Jayhawks traveled to South Bend, Indiana, to play the Notre Dame Fighting Irish on October 7, 1933, there was little hope among the KU faithful that the team had enough talent to compete with college football's elite program. It didn't matter that KU had already played and won two games—both shutout victories—or that Notre Dame had yet to play. The Fighting Irish had easily defeated the Jayhawks the year before in Lawrence, 24-6.

But somebody must have forgotten to tell the Jayhawks they were going to lose.

In one of the greatest efforts put forth by a KU football team, the gritty and seemingly outmanned '33 Jayhawks controlled the Irish for the duration of the game and earned a memorable 0-0 tie. *The Kansas City Star* ran this game recap the following day:

> *A powerful band of Jayhawkers from Kansas smashed Notre Dame tradition here this afternoon when they outfought and outplayed the Irish in the opening game of the year. Neither team scored, but it was Notre Dame which held Kansas to a tie and the Irish, at the end of the afternoon's vain effort, retired in confusion, demoralized as no Notre Dame eleven had been in many years.*
>
> *Only twice since the dark ages of football history, when Notre Dame lost an opening game in 1896, have the Irish been tied in their first contest.*

When the team returned from Indiana the following Monday, the student body was waiting at the train station to embrace their surprising football team. *The Star* reported the great celebration:

> *The University of Kansas football warriors, who morally conquered the Ramblers* (Notre Dame was also known as the Ramblers at that time) *of Notre Dame at South Bend Saturday. . .were met at the train here today by a student body which gave them the greatest reception ever received by the conquering heroes of the gridiron in the history of Mt. Oread.*
>
> *Displaying a huge sign, "We Whipped Notre Dame," and meaning every word of it, the students deserted classrooms, although no official holiday was declared. . .*

Kansas concluded the 1933 season with a 5-4-1 record, and also had the peculiar distinction of shutting out five of their opponents while *also* being shut out five times themselves. Notre Dame never recovered from its game with the Jayhawks and suffered one of its worst seasons ever to finish with a 3-5-1 record.

CHAPTER 2

Coming to Kansas—Recruiting Tales

"I fell in love with KU when I came up here for a visit. It was what I'd been looking for."

—Don Fambrough

The University of Kansas's football fortunes have always rested squarely on the shoulders of incoming recruits. While the Jayhawks have had little trouble attracting the best talent in the state of Kansas throughout the years, high school players and junior college transfers from New Jersey to California and Texas to Chicago have also come to KU to play football at the base of Mount Oread. While NCAA recruiting rules and regulations have rigidly affected recruiting practices for decades, the reasons a student-athlete comes to KU remain ever-changing—they are varied, engaging and sometimes amusing. Playing football at Kansas has always been a source of pride and passion for those who played at Memorial Stadium—several former KU players share their memories of how and why they became Jayhawks.

John Hadl, Quarterback (1959-61)

Perhaps the greatest all-around football player to ever play for Kansas, Hadl was the Jayhawks' first two-time All American. A great running back as a sophomore, the Lawrence, Kansas native, switched to quarterback his junior season and led the Jayhawks to the Big Eight title, and then to a Bluebonnet Bowl victory his senior year. Hadl was also an excellent defensive back, and his 98-yard interception return against TCU in '59 is still a KU record. Also an excellent punter, Hadl led the country in 1959 with a 45.6 average and holds the school record with a 94-yard boot against Oklahoma. As a runner he was balanced and elusive, as a passer sensational. Hadl had a 16-year career in the NFL, and is currently an associate athletic director at KU.

I had quite a few options on where I could go to play college football. Initially, when I started off, KU wasn't in a good coaching situation. I grew up in Lawrence and saw that whole bad state of affairs. I had made my mind up I was going to Oklahoma. I actually went down to Oklahoma on a visit and committed to Bud Wilkinson, OU's head coach. In the meantime, KU fired Chuck Mather (KU's head football coach, 1954-57) and hired

John Hadl. *University of Kansas Archives*

Jack Mitchell. Thank goodness, because when Jack came in, he got it all turned around in the right direction. In the long run it's obviously the best thing that ever happened to me, but I was headed for Oklahoma at one time.

Nolan Cromwell, Quarterback (1973-76)

The Jayhawks' greatest all-time rushing quarterback, the Ransom, Kansas, native guided KU's powerful wishbone offense for two seasons. Cromwell earned the 1975 Big Eight Offensive Player of the Year by rushing for 1,223 yards and nine touchdowns, and led Kansas to one of the biggest college football upsets of all time, a 23-3 win over Oklahoma. Originally a defensive back, the "Ransom Rambler" netted 126 tackles his first two seasons at KU. An honorable mention All-American in football, Cromwell earned All-America honors in track as well. A knee injury shortened his quarterback career at KU, but he still totaled 1,664 rushing yards in just 18 games. A second-round draft pick by the Los Angeles Rams, Cromwell played in the NFL until 1988. He is currently an assistant coach with the Seattle Seahawks.

I had narrowed things down to four schools: Oklahoma, Nebraska, KU and K-State. I took my visits to the other schools; the weekend we went to Oklahoma we had a huge snowstorm. Later on, toward the end of the recruiting season, I had pretty much made up my mind to go to Kansas because of the track program. Bob Timmons, KU's track coach, told me that he was going to let me do both if I chose to, and that if I wanted to quit one it didn't make any difference. Plus Coach Timmons said if I just wanted to run track that they'd give you a scholarship for that. Both sports had given me a good commitment and made me feel very good.

I was a quarterback and linebacker in high school, but I was recruited as a wide receiver. The first day of practice (1973)—I think it was the first year they let freshmen move up to varsity if they were good enough—they asked me if I wanted a chance to make the traveling squad as a freshman and I said sure. So they switched me to defensive back because they needed another person. I think about after the sixth game the starting free safety broke his arm, I went in and finished out the season.

David Jaynes, Quarterback (1971-73)

Mount Oread had never seen such a talented right arm. A native of Bonner Springs, Kansas, Jaynes came to KU as one of the most highly touted and recruited high school quarterbacks in the country. When he was done throwing passes for the Jayhawks four years later, he owned almost every passing mark in the school's record book. He finished with 5,132 career passing yards (broken by Frank Seurer) and 35 career touchdown passes, a record that still stands. His top single-game performance was against Tennessee in 1973: 35 of 58 attempts for 394 yards. Jaynes led the Jayhawks to the Liberty Bowl in '73, and earned All-America honors for himself—he also finished fourth in the Heisman Trophy balloting that year. Jaynes played in the NFL with the Kansas City Chiefs for one season.

The Kansas City Chiefs had just won the Super Bowl and the *Kansas City Star* came out with an article about me and how I was being recruited by colleges around the country. I'm at home when this article comes out and I get a phone call from Hank Stram, the Chiefs head coach. I was a ball boy with the Chiefs my junior and senior years in high school, so I had developed a nice relationship with Coach Stram. He's been a great guy over the years, and I still stay in touch with him. So Hank called and said, "It looks like you have a big decision to make." He asked me if I had anyone I could really talk to about it. My dad didn't have the background to give me input on the real issues. Stram told me to stop by his office and we would sit down to talk. We sat there for two hours going over the pros and cons of different schools and situations.

After our talk, we arrived at the decision that I should go to Alabama, and I made that decision. I actually signed a conference letter of intent, which is just binding within the conference. Once you sign, 30 days later the national letter of intent came out. I signed with Alabama with the full intention of going there. Then there were those 30 days where everyone went away, except Terry Donahue, who was the assistant coach at Kansas for Pepper Rodgers. During the whole recruiting process, Terry and I had really become friends. He stayed in contact with me, said he wanted to wish me luck at Alabama.

It was the day before the KU/K-State basketball game at Allen Fieldhouse and it was probably about 20 days after I signed the conference letter with Alabama. Coach Bryant (Alabama head coach) had been up to see me twice, so he really had some time invested in me. Anyway, Terry called and said he had an extra ticket for the basketball game— did I want to come up? I went to the game and I was just sitting in the fieldhouse with this incredible game going on. At that point, I thought "This is really where I want to be," and I told Coach Donahue that I was changing my mind. I wanted to go to KU. He took me up to Pepper's office immediately. Pepper said I was staying there that night, that they'd put me in a hotel. The next day they picked me up and I went to Pepper's office again. "The

David Jaynes. *University of Kansas Archives*

first thing we have to do is have you call Coach Bryant and tell him your decision," Pepper said. I told them I would do anything if they would just not make me call Coach Bryant and tell him that.

Pepper picks up the phone—and I know now, because he just told me recently—and dialed Bryant's phone number. But he didn't. He was pretending it was ringing, and he told me he wasn't there. Not too long ago I asked him if he really called Coach Bryant or if he was playing with me. Pepper laughed and told me he just wanted to make sure that I was serious about the decision to come to KU instead of Alabama.

Bill Whittemore, Quarterback (2002-03)

The heart and soul of the 2003 Jayhawks, Whittemore fought back from a shoulder/collar-bone injury and led the Jayhawks to their first bowl game in eight seasons. The Brentwood, Tennessee product was a tough runner and a precision passer. The Big 12's Offensive Newcomer of the Year in 2002, he broke KU's single-season touchdown pass record in '03 with 18, and added another 10 touchdowns on the ground. For his career Whittemore rushed for 1,083 yards and 21 touchdowns, and passed for 4,051 yards and 29 touchdowns.

I came out of junior college. I was getting some interest from different places, but then I got injured during my last regular-season game. I remember Purdue was kind of talking to me, but I wasn't really interested. My coach would tell me he was getting a bunch of calls, but I really tried to stay away from it to be honest, because I got the same thing in high school and I didn't want to deal with it in high school. You know, I had all kinds of schools calling me my senior year in high school, and they all seemed to kind of disappear around signing day, so I stayed away from it in junior college, too.

As soon as the season was over, I was talking to New Mexico and Middle Tennessee State. I was on my recruiting visit to New Mexico when Coach Mangino contacted me. He called my dad's cell phone and I told him I'd call him back because I was actually around the coaches at New Mexico at the time. Coach Mangino seemed like a nice guy, a straightforward guy, and honest. It seemed like he shot me pretty straight, telling me the situation I'd be in at KU and what kind of system he was bringing in. But I

Bill Whittemore. *University of Kansas Archives*

couldn't visit Lawrence before signing, and as it turned out, I ended up signing at Kansas before I even visited. And I never knew anything about Lawrence. I really didn't know much about Kansas football. I just knew that they hadn't been successful lately and that they were bringing in a new coach from Oklahoma.

Bert Coan, Running Back (1960)

One of the best running backs to ever grace the football field at KU, Coan was also one of the most controversial players in the school's history. A native Texan and transfer student from TCU, Coan had tremendous speed—he ran the 100-yard dash in 9.7 seconds—and had a bruising, six-foot-four, 200-pound body. He only played in seven and a half games for the Jayhawks but still led the team in rushing in 1960 with 488 yards and in scoring with 54 points. In 1961, Coan broke his leg in spring practice, missed the entire '61 season, and opted for the AFL's San Diego Chargers the following year. He also played for the Kansas City Chiefs from 1963-68.

I was kind of disenchanted at TCU (Coan attended TCU as a freshman), and hell, maybe I can get put in jail for this—but Bud Adams (owner of the then-Houston Oilers and KU alum) was getting ready to start the American Football League, he and Lamar Hunt, and Wilson out of Buffalo I guess. I think he was trying to get a jump on recruiting for the Oilers, I suppose, and he contacted me that summer to go to the College All-Star game in Chicago, and me being a young 18 year old, I didn't see anything wrong with it. We flew up to watch the game; I guess it was college all-stars against the NFL champs, and that would've been 1959 I guess. He said he'd heard I was dissatisfied at TCU, how he might've found that out, I don't know. He influenced me to go to KU, to transfer anyway. That's how it got started. I visited the campus. Jack Mitchell was the coach and he was pretty up front about everything, saying "If I was your parents, I'd kick your butt and tell you to go back to TCU." Something like that. He was a pretty funny guy.

Harrison Hill, Wide Receiver (1997-2001)

A great leaper with a soft pair of hands, Hill was an excellent receiver and punt returner. A product of Collegiate High School in Wichita, Kansas, he caught seven touchdown passes in his career and returned one punt for a touchdown. Hill's longest reception was a 62-yarder against Missouri in 1999. He pulled in 47 passes in 2000, and finished his career with 108 receptions for 1,535 yards. A shoulder injury and dehydration problems shortened Hill's career.

I didn't really grow up a huge KU fan. I didn't have any family that had gone there. Initially, when I was sophomore, junior in high school, Coach Mason recruited me, and the good thing about it was that my brother ended up transferring to KU. Once he transferred, I became a huge KU fan. I went there for a summer football camp before my senior year. That was really my first time there, and I talked to coaches and saw the campus. I totally loved the place. They offered me a scholarship at the summer camp. I was so excited because I had just ran a really good time, and even though it was just a summer camp, Coach Mason called me into his office that day and offered me a scholarship. It was the first scholarship I had been offered. I remember I ran to the phone and called my dad to tell him. He was so excited because my brother was a walk-on. The whole process was relatively easy because I was getting recruited hard by a lot of other Big 12 schools, but with my brother at KU, I wanted to be with him. That's pretty much what it came down to. I wanted to be with my brother and I loved KU. Plus, Kansas had been 10-2 the year before, and they went to the Aloha Bowl. I would be close to home, at a great school and get to talk to pretty girls on campus—it was everything I was looking for.

Mike Hubach, Punter/Place Kicker (1976-79)

One of KU's first true super kickers, the Cleveland, Ohio, native holds the Kansas career marks for most punting yardage with 10,618 yards, and most punts with 259. A two-time All-Conference selection in the Big Eight, Hubach was also a stellar field goal kicker. He booted three field goals of more than 50 yards in his career, and had career totals of 21 field goals and 72 PATs. He also led the Jayhawks in scoring all four seasons he played and finished with a career total of 135 points. Hubach was selected to play in the Japan Bowl All-Star game and Shrine Game following his senior season, and he played in the NFL with the New England Patriots for two seasons.

I remember sitting in class, I don't remember what subject it was, at West Tech High School in Cleveland, Ohio. The teacher pulled me out of a class and said someone's here to see you—it was Coach Vince Semary from Kansas (assistant coach at KU in 1975-76) and he told me his nephew wrestled at West Tech. He also told me he recruited city schools because you never knew what you might find there. So, I don't know if the guy was really in town visiting his family, or the nephew, or actually was recruiting, but he said he was from Kansas and that he wanted to talk to me. To be honest, I didn't know where Kansas was, geographically. I was thinking, Kansas, hmmm, it's out west somewhere. But if you put a map in front of me, I couldn't tell you where it was.

I was offered three scholarships: Kansas, Syracuse and Kentucky. Cleveland State offered me a soccer scholarship, but when I started visiting schools, seeing what a real college campus looked like, there was no way I was going to go to Cleveland State University. And to me, when I visited KU, it was a picture of what a college should really be like; the whole setting and all that, the old buildings, statues. And at Kansas, there was the opportunity to start right away my freshman year. I remember growing up and watching Nebraska and Oklahoma games on TV, and being able to play against those schools was an exciting thought. Plus, I got a sample of the food at the training table, and being able to eat that kind of food year round was a real positive, too.

Bobby Skahan, Quarterback (1964-66)

A fast runner who was also quick on his feet, the five-foot-10 Columbus, Kansas, native took over the quarterbacking duties for KU shortly after the start of his sophomore season. Skahan engineered the last-minute drive against Oklahoma in 1964 that resulted in a triumphant 15-14 win. Unfortunately, injuries severely limited his playing time his final two seasons at KU. Skahan led the Jayhawks in passing in '64 with 550 yards, and again in 1966 with 299 yards.

I visited a lot of different schools, but the only ones I took seriously were Missouri and Kansas. Jack Mitchell came down to visit me, and he was a great recruiter. He could talk you into about anything. Bud Wilkinson at Oklahoma was recruiting me as defensive back, and I didn't want to play defensive back. Jack told me he'd put me at quarterback. In high school I was a good running back, I was fairly quick. Jack liked that speed at quarterback, and that position didn't throw a lot in his offense. He also told me about Wilkinson leaving Oklahoma. I just thought he was blowing smoke at the time, but he did leave a year later. Jack was just a great recruiter, and I felt like KU had a real peace about it. It was a great place and a great campus. I was interested in the education part of it. I always felt it was a better school.

I decided that I wanted to play baseball also, which I did. They gave me a scholarship that no one else did. It was a football/baseball scholarship and I could choose which one to play after awhile. I wound up playing both. Kansas was a good opportunity for me. I actually got drafted after my sophomore year for baseball by the Yankees. I decided not to go on the draft and to stay at KU.

Emmett Edwards, Wide Receiver
(1972-74)

A world-class sprinter with a great pair of hands, Edwards broke every receiving record at KU during his career, and still ranks third on the school's all-time receiving yardage list with 1,808, and fourth on the all-time receptions list with 105. The Central High (Kansas City, Missouri) product put together his best season in 1973, catching 49 passes for 802 yards. He scored eight touchdowns in his career. A two-time

All-Conference selection in the Big Eight (1973-74), Edwards was a second-round pick by the Houston Oilers in the 1975 NFL draft, and he played two seasons in the league.

K ansas had an athletic department that was ou standing when I was being recruited. The high school I was at was known as a powerhouse in football, basketball and track—Central High School in Kansas City. KU during that time also had a good track and basketball team. They were outstanding. It seemed a good place to go, a place I would fit in. I was recruited by Missouri, K-State, the University of Tulsa and a few other small schools as well, but I knew Kansas was it for me.

Bobby Douglas, Quarterback, (1966-68)

A big, strapping southpaw out of El Dorado, Kansas, Douglas was as dangerous running the ball as he was throwing it. In 1968, his senior campaign, he led the Jayhawks to a share of the Big Eight Conference title and a spot in the 1969 Orange Bowl. He passed for touchdowns in six consecutive games in '68, still a school record, and finished his All-America season with 1,316 passing yards and 12 touchdown passes. For his career, Douglas had 2,817 passing yards and 20 touchdown passes. He was selected to play in the Senior Bowl, the American Bowl and the College All-Star Game following his senior season. A number-two draft pick by the Chicago Bears in 1969, Douglas played in the NFL for 13 seasons with the Bears, Chargers, Saints and Packers.

I was pretty highly recruited, on a regional basis, anyway. My brother was playing at Arkansas, they had gone to two Cotton Bowls in a row, and one of those years had tied for the national championship. They had really good football. But my brother never really started, and ended up going to Vietnam so he didn't get a chance to finish his football career there. Arkansas kind of thought they had me since my brother was in school there. I corresponded a lot with Arkansas and Missouri both. They really recruited me hard. Jack Mitchell, KU's coach, used to come down almost every week and take me to dinner, which in those days you could do. In those days, you didn't sign a letter of intent for your conference, but you really didn't sign the national letter of intent until May. I ended up really liking Jack Mitchell and decided I didn't want to go out of the state. I thought it would be advantageous to stay in Kansas. Of course, they hadn't had horrible football teams, yet. They were competitive. And, I think my Dad pushed me a little bit to KU. He really liked Jack Mitchell, too. Dad had quit coaching, and I think he wanted to watch. He didn't ever really say it, but he was happy that I was going to KU because it was close.

Spencer Bonner, Defensive Back (1991-95)

A tough, journeyman player most of his career at KU, the five-foot-11, 190-pound Bonner was a strong force on the Jayhawks' special teams his senior season. The Oak Park, Illinois, native set the tone for one of KU's biggest wins in 1995 when he blocked a punt against Colorado at Boulder early in the game.

I visited three schools. Kansas was the first, then I went to Minnesota, then Illinois. From there, I made a decision on what was available to me. Kansas was the best option for a lot of reasons. Minnesota was being investigated for some violations that happened when their prior coach was there. Illinois was only picking up two defensive backs that year, so they didn't offer right away, and Kansas already had an offer on the table. My mother was impressed with R.D. Helt and his recruiting tactics of keeping her informed on what the recruiting processes were. She really enjoyed that part. The other two schools didn't do that. So, she was really pulling for me coming to Kansas because she was informed as to what was going on. After looking at the overall situation, I decided that KU was going to be the best option. One, I didn't have to worry about violations and penalties with the NCAA like

Spencer Bonner. *KUAC Media Relations*

they did at Minnesota, and, of course, Illinois hadn't offered a scholarship. So, we called Kansas and told them I was coming.

Otto Schnellbacher, End (1942, 1946-47)

The "Double Threat from Sublette," Schnellbacher was a standout performer at Kansas in both football and basketball. A strong six-foot-three, 180-pound end on the gridiron, "Snelly" hailed from the small western Kansas town of Sublette, and is one of just three athletes to serve as captain for both the football and basketball teams. Schnellbacher was fast with a great pair of hands, and was also an exceptional blocker. He was just as good on the defensive side of the ball, and especially excelled on the special teams. Twice an All-Big Six selection in football (1946-47), he was named All-America in football in 1947. Schnellbacher finished his career at KU with 58 pass receptions for 1,069 yards—school records that stood for 22 years. He averaged 18.4 yards per reception. Schnellbacher played both professional football and basketball, and was an All-Pro defensive back three times.

In high school, I thought I was better at basketball because we'd won the state tournament. We were undefeated and I set a few scoring records. I was from a very small school (Sublette, Kansas) so we played 11-man football with about 18 players. We didn't have a chance to scrimmage much. We put our big kids from the farms in the middle of the line, and I was a linebacker on defense. We played well and won a lot of ball games, but when you have success in another sport that kind of leads you to basketball. I was recruited for basketball by Phog Allen. All the schools recruited me for basketball. None of them recruited me for football.

So I went to KU on a basketball scholarship. In those days we had jobs, and that was part of the scholarship. I had a job at the stadium, but I definitely wasn't going to go out for football. Then I got bumped—fired—from the job after I had been there for about a week, so I asked the foreman who fired me what I should do. He said "Go see Phog Allen." So I went to see Dr. Allen, who told me to go out for football so I could get the job back. And I did. I went out for football to make sure I had a job. What they'd done is two-time me. The football coaches had gotten together because they wanted me to go out for the team, and I had refused. So, they talked to Phog and figured out a way to get me to go out.

Don Davis, Linebacker (1991-94)

A rock-solid performer at the linebacker position for KU, the Olathe, Kansas native was a big reason the Jayhawks enjoyed a lot of winning success during his playing career. Davis garnered 79 total tackles in 1993, and twice was honored by the Big Eight as an Academic All-Conference selection. A free agent entry into the NFL, Davis has enjoyed a long, productive pro career, playing in the league for nine seasons.

I had four official visits during my recruiting process, and it really came down to KU and Missouri. I'm a big family guy, and all of my family lived close to Lawrence. Plus, KU just really had more of a family feel. The campus had a lot of appeal for me as well. All of the schools that were recruiting me were in about the same situation as far as the state of their respective programs, they were all sort of projecting what they were going to do in the future. Of course, coach Mason was an excellent recruiter. Mitch Browning, the linebackers coach, also recruited me, and he did an excellent job. It really just came down to the campus and being close to my family.

Mike Norseth, Quarterback (1984-85)

A juco transfer from Snow Junior College in Utah, the LaCrescenta, California, native was one of the biggest offensive weapons to ever play for KU. In just two seasons, the six-foot-three Norseth used his passing prowess to accumulate big numbers for the Jayhawks. He owns the school records for most completions in a season with 227, most passing yardage in a season with 2,995, most attempts in a season with 408, most passing yards in a game with 480, and he finished with 24 touchdown passes for his career. After playing in the 1985 Hula Bowl, Senior Bowl and Blue-Gray Classic All-Star games, Norseth was drafted by the Cleveland Browns in the seventh round of the 1986 NFL draft.

I was in junior college in Utah, and Coach Gottfried (KU's head coach, 1983-85) was actually looking at the quarterback from the year before me, and he saw me as well. That's kind of when it started. First, I looked at what Kansas had done the year before. Frank Seurer was the quarterback, and they threw the ball a lot. I grew up in Southern California, so I was kind of a Pac 10 guy. Really, my biggest thoughts of the Big Eight at the time were of Nebraska and Oklahoma. But with what Coach Gottfried was doing, I thought it was a chance to play at the highest level. I also thought that it was a place that I could go to and start right away, and follow behind Frank. It was a tremendous opportunity.

COMING TO KANSAS—RECRUITING TALES

Chip Hilleary, Quarterback (1989-92)

An all-around performer who excelled at both running and throwing the football, Hilleary was the Jayhawks' starting quarterback for three seasons. The Westerville, Ohio, product led the Jayhawks to their first winning season in a decade in 1991, and the school's first Bowl game victory since 1961 the following year. Hilleary finished his career at KU with 335 completions for 4,598 yards and 25 touchdowns. He was a Big Eight All-Conference selection, and Academic All-Conference pick his senior season.

My junior year of high school I never anticipated, never really thought about playing at the college level. Then I had a great senior year, and we had a great team. I was fortunate and stayed pretty healthy up until the last game. I was getting recruited by pretty much everybody like Ohio State and all the other major schools. Then I broke my shoulder in the state semifinals and that was last game of my high school career. Glen Mason was about the only coach from a major program who recruited me after that. I was first-team All-State and I couldn't even get the schools around there to talk to me after the injury, and it was on my non-throwing shoulder. Stories go back and forth about how Mitch Browning said he had to talk Coach Mason into even considering me. I was fortunate, though, and got to take return visits to KU. It was funny because Dana Stubblefield, who had a great career at Kansas, ended up being on the same Sunday/Monday trip that I took. He was a wrestler and had a meet on Saturday and I had a basketball game I had to participate in so we ended up taking an unusual Sunday/Monday trip to Lawrence. By the end of that trip I had committed to KU and canceled all my other visits.

Chip Hilleary. *KUAC Media Relations*

It's kind of a weird story, but it was the middle of the winter on the visit—a beautiful day in Lawrence. I really didn't know a whole lot about the Kansas tradition, not even the basketball tradition, other than that they had just won the National Championship. I had a cousin who went to KU and I just knew that she wore a Kansas sweatshirt around when we were growing up. That was the extent of what I knew about Kansas, but when I got there and looked at the education possibilities and got a chance to see the campus I was impressed. Coach Mason had a presence about him and I knew he was a winner. I knew he was somebody who was a strong power, someone that I knew I really wanted to play for. So I committed right away.

Max Ediger, Running Back (1974-78)

A gifted runner with blazing speed, Ediger was perfectly suited for KU's wishbone offense in the 1970s. The Topeka, Kansas, product put together a stellar season in 1977, gaining 443 yards rushing on 73 attempts for a 6.1 yards-per-carry average. Ediger had a 71-yard touchdown run against K-State that season, and he also pulled in seven passes for 120 yards. Originally a walk-on, he earned a full scholarship following his freshman year. A severe hamstring injury cost Ediger most of his senior season.

In high school, I had a lot of injuries. I broke my arm my sophomore year. My junior year, I got kicked in the kidney, and I was peeing blood for a couple games. Somebody had to help me after that. Every year, it seemed like there was something going on—I always had some kind of an injury. I never played in high school for a full year. My senior year in high school, I jumped on a football in the first game to recover a fumble and bruised a rib so bad I could hardly take a breath without it really hurting. So, for the next four or five games, I was really nursing that injury. As you can imagine, playing football while nursing a bruised rib was pretty tough, especially when you're trying to not show the pain. I'm sure that hurt my chances for a scholarship to a major school. It looked like I was probably a pansy because I was looking for a place to fall down. I had a 9.8 in the 100 coming off my junior year in track. Just that alone with a reasonable football year would have probably lead somewhere to a Division I school. Luckily, it didn't. Otherwise, I probably would have taken any four-year scholarship if I could have gotten it.

I actually did accept a scholarship to Ft. Scott junior college. But when I signed it, it was like "I've got to take something." I can't just throw away a scholarship. My Dad had died two weeks after I finished high school, so I was kind of searching. I didn't have him to lean on for advice—I was kind of on my own there. So I signed with Ft. Scott. The way I ended up at KU was, I really didn't want to go to Ft. Scott—I wanted to go to KU. Two weeks before the high school all-star game, I was contacted to play in the game in Wichita. The only reason they contacted me at all was because they remembered my speed in track. I guess the only reason I got invited so late was because they had a couple people who couldn't make it. So I ended up getting invited down there, which was really my ticket to KU because I ended up starting. You've got offense on the East team and an offense on the West, so right away, I was one of the two top running backs in the state, unless one of the players who was really good just didn't show up. Billy Campfield was playing for the West and I was playing for the East, and we both ended up at KU. Just based on my starting in the all-star game, one of KU's recruiting coaches came up to me after the game and said, "Hey, ever thought about walking on?" I said, "Sure, just tell me what day to be there." And that was it, that's how I ended up at KU—I really wanted to go there all along.

Moran Norris, Fullback (1996-2000)

A big, powerful and punishing runner, the six-foot-two, 245-pound fullback from Houston, Texas, started his career at KU as a tight end. When he was finally given a chance to run the ball on a regular basis his junior season, he bashed out 537 yards and eight touchdowns on the ground. Injuries

*severely hampered his senior year, but Norris still gained 313
yards rushing that season. He was drafted by the New Orleans
Saints in the fourth round of the 2001 NFL draft, and has
played three years in the league.*

Kansas had just defeated UCLA in the Aloha Bowl,
beat them pretty good. I thought they had an
excellent program, they had a high rate of players graduating—KU was my first choice. But almost all of the Big 8
schools were looking at me, and there were some black colleges that wanted me, too. And Arkansas. Still, there
weren't as many schools as I thought there would be. It's
kind of funny because when I came out of high school—I
was playing tight end—a lot of the recruiters were actually coming to see our quarterback. But at the game they
were watching, I did really well, and they started looking
at me.

Ray D. Evans, Defensive Back (1978-81)

*The son of KU great Ray Evans, the Rockhurst High
(Kansas City, Missouri) graduate excelled on special teams
and was a solid performer in the defensive backfield for the
Jayhawks. An intelligent player and hard hitter, Evans suffered a knee injury that shortened his career.*

I actually thought hard about going somewhere else
to play college ball. It was kind of that 18-year-old
deal where I wanted to blaze my own trail a little bit.
Believe it or not, I really liked Iowa State, and I liked their
coaching staff a lot, too. They had a guy named Jim
Williams who was an assistant coach, and he was recruit-

Ray Evans. *University of Kansas Archives*

ing Kansas City well at the time. Plus, they actually had put together a sting of 8-3 seasons. So I liked them, and I also liked Iowa. I thought very hard about that. But in the end, it was just too ingrained in me about what I would do. The reality was I wanted to go KU—it had been deep in my blood for a long time.

Marlin Blakeney, Defensive Back (1991-95)

The Leavenworth, Kansas, native developed into a good performer in the defensive backfield for the Jayhawks. the five-

foot-11, 190-pound Blakeney fought through injuries the first part of his career and was also a strong force on KU's special teams. He recorded 37 total tackles in 1993 and intercepted a pass against Alabama-Birmingham.

I came out of Leavenworth, Kansas, and my high school coach was close to Coach Mason and the rest of the KU coaching staff. He would send us to summer camp every year and he'd come along with us. That's how it used to be. I fell in love with KU because Coach Mason and all the coaches really worked with me in camp. I really took advantage of the time they had with me. They kept in touch with me throughout the year. But, I also was recruited by Missouri, and I think that was the first trip I took. They showed my Mom a good time, and they've got the third-ranked journalism school in the country—or something like that. So, that was kind of appealing. Then I went to K-State, and that was right when Bill Snyder came in. They were really, really interested in having me out there. They had everything I could want, but the key was that I honestly fell in love with KU. I didn't take any more trips after that. I decided to go to KU probably a week or two after that. The other coaches were mad, too. The MU coach called and pretty much cussed me out on the phone.

L.T. Levine, Running Back (1992-95)

An important weapon in KU's offense for most of his career, Levine put together a solid record on the football field at Kansas. A standout high school star from Colonia, New Jersey, he ran for more than 800 yards his junior and senior seasons at KU. Levine scored 22 touchdowns and finished his career with 2,248 rushing yards, seventh best in Kansas history. He played in the Shrine Game at San Francisco following his senior season, and was drafted by the Denver Broncos in the seventh round of the 1996 NFL draft. Levine played one season with the Broncos.

I was just like most of the other recruits, I took five visits. My mother would go one week before me to visit each campus and give me a report before I visited. She really liked Kansas, and when I got there it pretty much just confirmed everything she said. My host was Kyle Moore, and his roommate was Gilbert Brown. He was the biggest human being I had ever seen in my life at that time. They just showed me around and made me feel at home. The great thing about it was it was the week before Christmas break, and a lot of kids were gone and I still had a good time. It was what you might call trouble nowadays, but it was just innocent fun.

Curtis McClinton, Fullback (1959-61)

A hard, pounding runner, punishing blocker and fine receiver, "Tank" McClinton was a three-time All-Big Eight selection and an All-American in 1961. A product of Wichita North High School, the six-foot-three, 227-pound fullback led the Jayhawks in rushing in 1959 with 472 yards, and in pass receptions in 1960 and 1961. McClinton completed his career at KU with 1,377 rushing yards. Also a standout performer in track, McClinton was a three-time Big Eight high hurdles champion. Following his senior campaign, he played in the East-West Shrine game, the Hula Bowl and the College All-Star game. Drafted in the 14th round of the 1962 AFL draft by the Dallas Texans (now the Kansas City Chiefs),

McClinton earned Rookie of the Year honors in 1962. He played in two Super Bowls, and was a member of the Chiefs' 1970 Super Bowl Championship team.

I graduated from North High in Wichita, Kansas with a lot of opportunities being an All-American in football and All-State hurdle champion. But, I fell in love with KU the first time I saw the campus when I went to the Kansas Relays. I cannot tell anyone how impressive it is when you are a young kid and you see the first hill in Kansas, especially as flat as that state is. I fell in love with the place. Also, I had success there at the relays in high school and I ran in the junior Olympics there at KU. I had a passion for KU.

Now, getting there was a little bit more complex. Chuck Mather was the football coach and I did interact with him. But, I ended up going one year to the University of Wichita (now Wichita State) because that's the school my sixth grade teacher—and my mentor—Lynwood Sexton attended. At that time, Coach Fambrough was also there. Jack Mitchell had just left and gone to Arkansas. So, I ended up there at Wichita for one year. Also, my dad was the state senator for the state of Kansas and there was some influence in that area. Eventually, I continued to follow my heart. I left the University [of Wichita] after my freshman year, went into the service for six months and ended up with Coach Jack Mitchell and Coach Fambrough at KU.

Kerwin Bell, Running Back (1980-83)

A part of one of the most ballyhooed recruiting classes in the history of KU, Bell traveled to Mount Oread from Huntington Beach, California, to become a Jayhawk. A five-

Curtis "Tank" McClinton. *University of Kansas Archives*

foot-nine speed burner, he had great instincts and was an exceptional open-field runner. Bell had a brilliant freshman season, gaining 1,114 rushing yards and scoring seven touchdowns, a performance that him earned Big Eight Offensive Newcomer of the Year, as well as being selected for the All-Conference team. After battling injuries his sophomore and junior seasons, Bell ran for 498 yards his senior campaign. He finished with 1,970 rushing yards for his career.

After taking all my recruiting trips, which were to Texas, Oklahoma, USC and Nebraska, John Hadl was in California visiting Frank Sauer, who had signed to go to KU. He asked Frank about me and Frank said no, Kerwin hasn't made up his mind yet. So they got together and asked me if I wanted to take a trip to KU. I said sure. So I ended up taking a trip to Kansas, and I enjoyed it. I knew about Coach Hadl from his days in San Diego. Bill Malavasi, who was also at our high school, had committed to Kansas, too. His father was the head coach of the Rams at the time. Our high school team won the state championship, and we were pretty good friends; me, Frank, Bill Malavasi and Mark Boyer were pretty much the nuts and bolts of the team. Frank and Bill were on me to go to KU. One thing led to another, and I really thought about it. My mother was pulling me in one direction—she wanted me to go to Texas—and my father was pulling me in a different direction—he wanted me to go to USC. I just said the heck with it—I'll go with Bill and Frank to Kansas and try to make something happen, try to help turn the program around. I felt football was football. At that time, you still had your powerhouses. I knew with my talent and Frank and Bill's talent—coupled with guys like Mike Arbanas—that maybe we could do something special.

Jason Thoren, Linebacker (1994-97)

The hard-hitting Lawrence, Kansas, native put together a superb defensive career for the Jayhawks. The six-foot-two, 230-pound Thoren pounded opposing runners throughout his stint at KU, and had his finest season in the Jayhawks' great 1995 season, collecting 119 tackles, three interceptions and two fumble recoveries. The Associated Press made him a second-team All-Conference selection in 1995. For his career, Thoren tallied 303 tackles and four interceptions.

I had the opportunity to go to other schools, but for me it was always KU. I grew up in Lawrence, and I followed the team growing up. It was right at the point when they were starting to show some signs of becoming a good team. They had some big-time players in the program, and they were a lot of fun to watch. I loved watching them when they were going 1-10 or 2-9 every year. Of course, the group right before me had Gilbert Brown and Dana Stubblefield. Just a solid group of players, and really, they were on the up and up. It was a no-brainer for me to choose KU.

Chip Budde, Center (1986-90)

Another Lawrence, Kansas, son who played a big role in turning around the Jayhawks' football fortunes, the six-foot-two, 265-pound center was the essence of durability, reliability and fortitude on KU's offensive line for four seasons. Budde started in 44 consecutive game for the Jayhawks—almost unheard of for an offensive lineman. Following his senior season, Budde was selected for the Blue-Gray All-Star Game at Montgomery, Alabama.

I wasn't really heavily recruited out of high school. I talked to Iowa, Minnesota, and made some stupid attempts to get into an Ivy League school—I actually generated some interest from Harvard, but it really came down to Colorado and KU. Gary Barnett was my recruiter out of Colorado, he was the assistant coach who was responsible for recruiting me. I went out there for a visit and met Coach McCarthy and really didn't hit it off with the guy, there was really no connection there, and I really didn't feel that he was the type of guy that I wanted to spend five years of my life with—the way he ran his football program, it kind of cleared my decision out. Bob Valesente took the head coach position at KU the winter of my senior year, Gottfried left and went to Pittsburgh. Kansas went 6-6 in 1985, but should have done a lot better, they lost a really close one down at Florida State, and everything kind of went to pot from there for the team after Gottfried left.

I'm convinced that Bob Valesente offered me a scholarship simply because Colorado did, and he didn't want to lose a hometown guy to another school, just because they offered a scholarship. And it worked out for the best, I couldn't be happier with my decision. But he was new at that point. Obviously you know he was a lot more in touch with wanting to be an upstanding member of the community. He wanted to be a Joe Paterno of Kansas. He wanted to be here for 50 years.

Charlie Hoag, Running Back (1950-52)

Another stellar two-sport athlete, Hoag came to KU from Oak Park, Illinois. In addition to playing football, he also played on KU's 1952 national championship basketball team,

Charlie Hoag. *University of Kansas Archives*

and was a member of the 1952 Olympic basketball team. Hoag fought injuries throughout his career at KU but was an instrumental member of the football team as KU won 21 games in his three years of playing time. In 1952, Hoag led the team in rushing with 469 yards, and also receptions with 16 for 380 yards as he was named to the Big Seven All-Conference team.

I went to Oklahoma and I met Jack Mitchell when he was still at Oklahoma, and I was totally impressed. And I was really going to go to Oklahoma, and I told my folks and they were so upset, because they wanted me to go to Kansas. They wouldn't express it until I wanted to go to Oklahoma, and they weren't happy. I went to bed that night and had trouble sleeping because they were so upset. I got up the next morning and told them I was going to Kansas and the press got ahold of it and it was in the paper and that was it. And I'm glad I did. Football-wise, I probably would have been better off at Oklahoma, but overall, basketball and everything, being able to go to the Olympics and playing on the national championship team, it was much better for me at KU.

CHAPTER 3

The Great Players

"Gale was a very unselfish player. I was always intrigued by that, because he was so talented. He could do it all. He was the best player in the nation, and it's sad he didn't win the Heisman Trophy."

—Bobby Skahan, on Gale Sayers

Superb, talented athletes have always played football at the University of Kansas. From Otto Schnellbacher to Bill Whittemore, Jayhawk fans have been able to witness some of the finest players in the country on the field at Memorial Stadium. And what makes a player celebrated and unforgettable usually goes beyond physical talent. KU has had several student athletes who can be defined as great—that special player who not only is the best on the Jayhawks' squad, but also the best player on the field in every game he plays. A common thread among the Jayhawk greats is that they invariably have the uncanny knack of making their teammates better, too.

Otto Schnellbacher on Ray Evans

Ray Evans held all the offensive passing records for years at KU before they started changing the system and throwing it like in basketball. I thought his greatest ability was his defense. He's probably the best defensive halfback that I saw, even in my pro days. Ray made the play when it had to be made. If something big had to happen on either offense or defense, Ray was going to be the person who did it. If you needed to have a tackle made, Ray was the person who did that. We were playing Missouri and I saw their fullback go up the middle, and I thought, "Oh my God, he's gone." Ray was across the field and caught him on the 10-yard line. I don't know how he caught him, but he caught him. That was in 1947.

In 1946, against Missouri, he goes back to throw right before halftime—they're playing a pass defense—and he tucks it down to run and we all knew what that meant—get your body on somebody. We make a couple blocks for him, he went 54 yards for touchdown, and we go into the half ahead. Missouri was a good ball club in those days—they were tough. Nebraska, Oklahoma and Missouri were the real tough ball clubs. If you got by those three games, you won the conference.

Ray Evans. *University of Kansas Archives*

David Jaynes

Not many people remember this, but my senior season I didn't have a Jayhawk logo on my helmet. I had concussion problems when I was playing high school football, and also in college. Riddell, the helmet company, had a helmet out where you put an air thing in it and pumped it up. It was supposed to be the latest, greatest helmet. My senior year at Kansas I decided to use that type of headgear—the rest of the team had these different, padded helmets. The Jayhawk logo on their helmets was underneath an acrylic part of the helmet—the decals weren't applied at KU, they were applied at the manufacturer. The Riddell helmet was just a blue helmet without any decals on it, so I wore it without the Jayhawks. I didn't really think about it or care about it. It didn't matter to me.

Jack Mitchell, Head Coach (1958-66) on John Hadl

The last coach to lead the Jayhawks to an undisputed league title (later forfeited), Mitchell also led KU to a Bluebonnet Bowl victory in 1961. His overall record at Kansas was 44-42-5.

John Hadl was a halfback at Lawrence High, and he said himself that he'd made his mind up to go to OU. My priority was Kansas boys, and the number-one player in the state of Kansas was right there in my backyard—and he was going to go to OU. You couldn't have anything worse than to have that guy go to Oklahoma, and we couldn't have that. The kid was born to be a quarterback. He was a natural leader, the players loved him, and he was right there in Lawrence. He had all the talent and ability for an option quarterback and he was a natural passer. You could see that before practice. They would go out there and play catch and he could flip the ball behind his back. He just had hands. Natural coordination to throw the ball, but he hadn't done much throwing. That was probably one of the best things that happened for us was to get John. He's just a great athlete.

Mike Norseth

I think Richard Estell and I certainly had a connection. I don't know what kind of numbers he ended up with. In the offensive scheme that Coach Gottfried was running, you tried to do everything in order of reading the defense and figuring out what is going to be the best opportunity based on the play you have. But, I think that any quarterback would tell you at certain times if you can get one receiver somewhat in the scheme of what you were trying to do quicker than the others, Richard was probably that guy.

Jack Mitchell on Gale Sayers

There were a lot of things involved with the recruiting process. Gale Sayers was probably the most sought after high school player in the United States at that time. He had speed, won every 100-yard dash he ran in. He was probably the fastest back in the country. Most kids with speed like Sayers had grown up with intramural, small-time, sandlot football, and they'd just outrun everybody. They had that speed all their lives so they'd just take the ball and outrun everybody. They don't learn how to cut. They don't learn how to weave. They don't know how to get out of tight spots. Then, when they get in college, all they can do is outrun people and that's not good enough. There are a lot of college guys who can run, but that won't cut the mustard. As far as running the ball, 90 percent of the guys cannot cut and weave because they've never done it. But Sayers was able to do that. I don't know how he learned it, but he was able to control his speed. It was just natural.

I spent a lot more time with him than I did with a normal recruit. Our program was a little better at that time than Nebraska's. We had a little more excitement. Having Kansas City close to the school was a big plus. I used Kansas City, and I used their alumni. Any big business in Kansas City, you get a kid from KU who has a degree in business or whatever and is an All-American, that's an asset to your business. If you can hire that guy, you've got a pretty good product. So, I took him to KC and went to three or four of the top businesses, and they were all KU alums, of course. I showed him the potential, the possibility—you get a degree in business from KU, you've got a position here. Not just him, for anybody from KU who's got a degree and if they want to go to work and especially if they have a big name. You're doing them a favor more than they're doing you a favor to have access to a kid like that. I did that with several players.

Max Ediger on Billy Campfield and Laverne Smith

I backed up Billy Campfield for my first couple years. He was a tremendously great blocker, and I don't

Gale Sayers, the Kansas Comet. *University of Kansas Archives*

know if very many people remember that. He was a great athlete in general—very fast and probably one of the strongest guys, pound for pound, on the team. He wasn't a real big runner, though, and he was only about 195 pounds at he most.

Laverne Smith probably did not lift a lot of weights. I think Laverne was the fastest athlete I've ever been around on any sport level. A lot of people don't realize this, but he was two-tenths off the world record in the hundred meters in track. I think the record was 9.9 and he ran a 10.1, something like that—a step off from the world record. He was a world-class sprinter. On the field, he could just turn on a dime and would be gone. When he ran, it looked so effortless, like he was cruising. You had no idea how fast he was really running.

Harrison Hill on Bill Whittemore

Bill was my roommate for a year, and I know him pretty well. There were a couple of things I wish I could change about my career. I loved my quarterbacks, but I wish that I could've played with Bill because he was the kind of guy who's tough, plays with a lot of heart and he'd do anything for his teammates. He'd do anything to win. He had talent, but he's the kind of guy who everyone wants to root for. The sort of guy who would go out on one leg and do everything that he could to win the game. I could tell that about him when he first came—I hosted him on his visit to KU. We became buddies, and I remember before we were living together, going into his junior year he wasn't the starting quarterback. I remember Bill would come home after two-a-days and be frustrated. He felt like he was playing good and he was upset. He should've been. I told him he had to hang in there. He's a game player. In practice, Bill looks okay, but not like an All-American. The stuff Bill does you can't really see in practice. I told him his time would come and to keep battling. Bill got a shot and as soon as he got in there, you knew he was a gamer. I thought he was good, but nobody knew how good he was until he got into the game. He does whatever it takes, and I'd rather have Bill than any other quarterback out there.

We had guys who could make plays, but Bill was everything to them. He was the leader. You could tell by watching him that people believed in him. The players did, the fans did, the coaches did—you just think of Bill as a winner. There's no way you can tell me that when it's the fourth quarter and we're down by ten and Bill's not in there, you're doubting yourself a little more. If he's in there, you think somehow you'll win. When he's not there, you don't have that same feeling.

Curtis McClinton

The environment at KU was totally compatible to academic achievement and learning. You get on campus and you get your head in a book. After the book, you go to practice. I was a double major in business and education. I also had a strong minor in music and voice. I spent most of my time either in the practice room with voice or piano, or studying at the library in the stacks. KU had a very accommodating attitude in regard to fraternities, and I was in the same fraternity that Wilt Chamberlain was a part of. All the guys were part of that fraternity. Dave Harris, Homer Floyd, these were some of the African-American guys who came in with Chuck

Mather. We had a very dynamic social life. In the midst of that, if you drop a shoe in the middle of a pail, it was a different environment then in regard to our society. Kansas has always been a free state, and I've always felt comfortable. My dad, the first black senator in the state of Kansas, backed civil rights legislation and public accommodations in 1955. It took him until 1958-59 to get it passed. There was a metamorphosis that was taking place at that time.

I've always said that being at KU was like being in a cocoon. It was a soothing environment in reference to the rest of the world. I wasn't the best student, but I maintained a B average. I feel very proud of that, because it's one of the best universities. When I went and did my grad work at Michigan and finished up with an A average, I felt I really had that foundation here from KU. Also, I matured. The social environment? The university allowed you to make choices regarding friends, people, sororities and fraternities, girlfriends, guy friends and people whom you like. The environment was good. The times—the rest of the world—outside of that cocoon, was a very segregated world. There were a lot of people at that particular time who made life very easy on the football field. Coach Mather brought a couple of black players onto the football team, and I don't think at that time that Kansas had had that many black ball players.

Jack Mitchell on Curtis McClinton

Curtis McClinton is one of the greatest! He is one of my favorite kids. Curtis was at Wichita North High School when I was at Wichita State, before I went to Arkansas. Well, there's Curtis, one of the best players in the state right out of Wichita High, and I gave him the working over. We spent a lot of time with him, and he liked us. His mother was a school teacher there. He comes from a very nice family. His mother was a well-educated and nice woman, and she wanted her boy at home. I spent some time with her recruiting Curtis, and it looked like we were in good shape with him, but then he went into the service for a year or so. Of course, KU was after him also. In the meantime, I went to Arkansas and then came to KU. I got a call from a good friend of mine in Wichita, one of the top KU alums we had down there. He was a big KU supporter. He told me, "There's a player down here who has been in the service, and he was a good high school player. You might be interested in him, and I know his family." I asked who it was. "I don't know if you know him or not, but his name is McClinton." I said yes, I know him. I know him well, and he knows me, too. He said, well, he's back. I said, "Oh my God, we've got to get him. He's a top player, a top student and a beautiful singer. He's a top player in every respect. He's a Kansas kid, and we've got to have him." And we went out after him.

Max Ediger on Nolan Cromwell

Nolan Cromwell is the type of guy who no matter what type of sport you were playing, if you were going to play tiddly winks or anything, he was the type of guy you would always want on your team because he could master it so quickly, so easily. He broke the decathlon record as a freshman at KU. I remember Fambrough talking about him. I guess he was on a some kind of trip and Cromwell was with him. I think all the coaches were playing golf and Nolan said, "Coach, I've never even had a golf club in my hand." I guess one of the coaches took him to

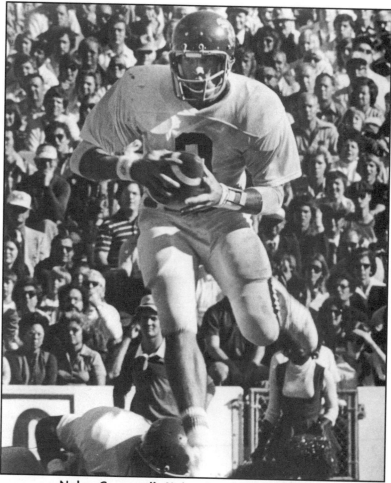

Nolan Cromwell. *University of Kansas Archives*

the side and showed him how to hold it, how to swing it. By the end of the round, I think Nolan was at least equal to all the other players—the first time he ever played the game. He was just a gifted athlete.

Don Fambrough on the '68 Team

Those kids on the 1968 team, Zook, Douglas, Riggins, were probably the greatest group of football players that we've ever had here at the University of Kansas at one time. I get kind of upset sometimes when I hear people say that you can't win with Kansas kids. My opinion in recruiting is that you always want to get the nucleus of your freshman class from your home state. I think it's very important that you strive to do that. I know you can't get them all, but we tried. We don't have that type of population. But that football team with Zook and Douglas and Riggins and all that crowd, 10 out of the starting 11 were from the state of Kansas. And they did pretty well. They went to the Orange Bowl and should have won if we'd had somebody here who could count. We

Bobby Douglas. *University of Kansas Archives*

had 12 people on the field you know, and that's what cost us the game. But, oh that was a fine football team. It was excellent. And I tell you, they played hard on the field, and they played hard off the field, too.

Chip Hilleary on Tony Sands

Touchdown Tony Sands. You talk about a guy having the biggest heart for the smallest body that I've ever seen. He reminded me of a pendulum, he was like a weeble-wobble—you could never get him down. He had the best balance that I've ever seen, but his work ethic and his heart are what I remember Tony for. The 1991 Missouri game, basically, reflected everything that Tony Sands stands for. To be able to take the beating that he took the day of Missouri game, and to get as many yards out of such a small body and such short legs—incredible. He put on more yards that day, which was one of the more impressive performances I've ever seen. The length of the football field—he ran it four times, and the average tailback averages probably 60-70 yards a game. He almost got 400 yards. It's just hard to believe.

In the course of the game, I lost track of how many times he carried the ball and how many yards he was getting—until the fourth quarter. I could have sat at the line of scrimmage, told the Missouri guys where we were going to run Tony to, what play it was going to be, and they still wouldn't have been able to stop us. Give credit to Tony, but also to the offensive line that was in front of us. Chris Perez playing at tackle and Keith Loneker, the other tackle. Hempstead, Schmidt and probably John Jones. That's where all the credit went. Tony was definitely the piece of the puzzle to make it all complete, but it all started with those guys. That reflected what Glenn Mason football was all about. Smash-mouth football. We probably had 500 and some total offensive yards. I would say Tony ran 396. I know I had 80-some yards that day running. So we probably had 600 yards total offense. I just think of Tony, I can picture it still today, Perez carrying him on his shoulder off to the sideline and the exhaustion he was in, but that was the way he went out. That was the way you remember Tony Sands. He went out on top.

Kelly Donohoe, Quarterback (1986-89) on Tony Sands

A scrappy, determined quarterback for a couple of KU's lesser teams, Donohoe nonetheless performed at a high level throughout his tenure with the Jayhawks. A product of Harrisonville, Missouri, he threw for 411 yards against Iowa State in 1989, the second-best single-game total in KU history. For his career, Donohoe amassed 5,382 passing yards—second all time at Kansas—and 24 touchdown passes. He is currently the head football coach at Blue Springs High School in Missouri, where his teams have won two of the last three state championships.

Tony Sands was one of the most interesting characters I've ever been around. I remember Tony in the elevators his freshman year. I'd just got there for two-a-days, and he had his sweat suit on. He was all of about 5'5"—short, but he was a talker. And I'm thinking "Who is this little joker? Why did they recruit this guy?" It wasn't long before we knew why.

Tony was a really a special player. My senior year, his sophomore year, in the huge game against K-State where we won, Tony had a big day, rushing for over 200 yards. He was all heart and hard muscle, and it really changed my perspective as a coach today. You don't need a big guy. You need a guy who has a lot of heart and strength and determination. Tony could hide back there behind all those big linemen, and that's what he did a lot. Tony and I shared a lot of time together in our dorm, and there were some hilarious moments with him, pranks that were pulled back and forth between us.

Tony Sands is carried off the field after his record-breaking day. *University of Kansas Archives*

John Hadl

We had a crazy bunch of guys who hung out together during the off season, a lot of guys who drank beer and raised hell. You know, typical stuff. They were good guys who didn't get in trouble, but we had the usual fights. In those days, you had a fistfight. Not that I did any of that, but some of those linebackers had the mentality to get into it once and a while.

I was sitting downtown in one of the college bars, sitting with this girl by the front window and talking to her. This guy kept coming over and trying to hustle her right in front of me. I finally told him to back off. He came back again, and this teammate of mine, Mike Fisher, was standing there. I said "Mike, get this guy out of here." I turned my back, and the next thing I know I see this object fly over my head right through the plate glass window. The guy got up and stumbled off and I never saw him again. I didn't mean for Fisher to do that, but that's what he did. Mike was older than everyone. He'd been in the marines already and had come back to school. He ended up being an academic counselor at Kansas—IQ of about 200.

Jack Mitchell on Bert Coan

He was a sweet boy, really. A very shy, backward type of a kid and very loyal. A fine, fine young man, no question about it. And, a great, great, great runner. It's a shame he broke that leg. If Bert hadn't broken that leg, he would have been one of the greatest pro players in the country. He broke his shin bone. It was a compound fracture. It was a terrible thing. After that, he just couldn't do the things he did before.

Pepper Rodgers, Head Coach (1967-70) on John Riggins

As the head coach of the Jayhawks, Rodgers will always be remembered for taking KU to the Orange Bowl following the 1968 season.

John Riggins is one of the legends in football. We had a player the year before, J.C. Hixson, who was the fullback and weighed 175—a wonderful human being. He played his ass off. But the fullback was a key guy. Then of course, John started playing in 1968 and he was 235 pounds and had won the Kansas State 100-yard dash championship. He's in the Hall of Fame. Riggins made a tremendous difference on our team.

There was another guy who made a huge difference and wasn't really recognized. His name was Larry Brown. He was a left tackle one year; he was a tight end one year and a defensive end one year. He was a four-time pro-bowler, won four Super Bowl rings playing tackle for the Pittsburgh Steelers. At that time there were not a lot of black athletes in the South. He was from Florida. We were able to go down and bring him up to play for us. You've got to have a few stars. You've got to have a John Riggins. You've got to have people who make a difference.

Harrison Hill on His Teammates at KU

Roger Ross started with me for a couple years, I think. He came in from a junior college and the first time I saw him running in practice I knew this guy would be great. He was short, wasn't extremely fast, but he

John Riggins. *University of Kansas Archives*

was an unbelievably smooth receiver and a tough kid. I remember having so much fun playing with him because he was a guy I learned a lot from, how he ran routes. I didn't really feel like I had a lot guys to learn a ton from and just the way he ran was always something nice to watch. The best thing about Ross was that he came in very behind on academics, but he got offered a scholarship, got a chance to go to a big university, and I've never seen a guy work harder in my life than he did. He was in the classroom, with tutors every single night for hours to get a college degree and he got it. It totally changed his life. Guys like Andrew Davison, I knew he got a lot of crap in college for being cocky, saying stuff in the papers, but he was one of the toughest competitors I ever went up against in practice in my whole college career. Even more, he was just like Roger; went to a terrible school, was in gangs as a kid, but realized that by going to KU he had a chance to do something with himself. That may not be football related, but to me those are the guys who I respect the most and would do anything for at this point because they had to work harder than the average Joe did to get through college.

The thing I loved about college football at KU, the best thing about it is taking a bunch of guys from tons of different backgrounds and putting them in a group. Guys who probably wouldn't have associated with each other in a different setting all become one. They become a family and they become best friends. That's the best part. That's the biggest learning experience; to become best friends with someone who has absolutely nothing in common with you except a desire to win. That desire to win, that desire to work brings you together and makes you friends. It builds a bond that nobody can break. I don't care if I don't talk to these guys in 20 years, if I saw Andrew Davison today I would do anything for him.

Don Fambrough, Guard (1946-47); Head Coach (1971-74, 1979-82)

A two-time All-Big Six standout as a player and the Big Eight Coach of the Year as the Jayhawks' head man, Fambrough's loyalty and love for the Jayhawks runs true and deep. As a player, Fam helped KU to a two-year record of 15-3-3. His overall record as Kansas's head coach was 36-49-5.

Ray Evans was the greatest football player I've ever been around. He had it all. I remember the first time I heard the saying "Lead by action rather than words," I thought to myself, whoever said that had Ray Evans in mind. He wouldn't say maybe three words the entire football game, but he was the type of player who, when we heard his number called in the huddle, was going to run with the ball or he was going to throw the ball and you wanted to do just a little bit extra because you knew he would give 110 percent. He was just an outstanding athlete. He could run, he could block, he could play defense, and he was a tremendous leader. So if I was starting out today, right now, and I had my first choice of picking from every football player I've ever known or ever played with or against, Ray Evans would be my first choice.

Gale Sayers was the greatest running back I've ever known. Nolan Cromwell was a great athlete. But Ray Evans was number one. He was head and shoulders above anyone I've ever been associated with. Otto Schnellbacher was a tremendous receiver. He played professional football with the New York Giants and also played defensive safety. And I never will forget that the first time I heard about that, I was really shocked, but here recently, I was looking up in some kind of sports book and I saw that when he was playing with the Giants he made all-pro. So he was a tremendous athlete. Now back to Ray, I don't know if you knew, he made All-America in both football and basketball. I don't think very many people have ever done that. Now Otto played both sports and was great, too. He and I were co-captains of the Orange Bowl team. But Ray Evans is the best athlete and best player I've ever been associated with, and one of the best people, too.

Nolan Cromwell on
Becoming a Wishbone Quarterback

I ran track during spring ball. I would do my track workout, then come over and usually get to the football fields about halfway through the practice. Then I would suit up and start doing drills with the defensive backs. I think the first week of spring ball, the defensive back coach told me to go see Coach Moore. He said he'd like to take a look at me at the quarterback position. If it works, great, but if it doesn't, then I'd definitely be a starter in the secondary. And it didn't matter to me where I played. I was too dumb to understand anything else. Whatever the coach said, I would do it, I didn't look at it any other way. They knew I would be able to play there without a problem. We went that way, and for me, I got a lot of attention, a lot of notoriety for playing quarterback.

I don't think I had a question whether I could do it or not. I felt like I could do anything. I played quarterback in high school, so I didn't think it was a big deal. Just going through the progression and understanding what the wishbone offense was all about was different. It was more suited to my abilities. But I was not a passer. We worked on passing about ten minutes a day during the year.

Everything else was running the ball. I ended up running the wishbone and doing the things that I could do well—run the ball. I don't think there was ever a question in my mind that I could do it. Now, could I do it better than anyone else on the team? That was their decision to make.

Bill Whittemore

My game is more mental than anything. The other guys are getting pumped up and jumping around and all, but I definitely picture it, because my mental preparation is about knowing my role, knowing my text. I don't picture plays as much as I picture the other team's defense, I guess—what they're going to do against me and what I'm going to do to alter our play when they do something. You also have to picture it in a positive way, visualize throwing for first downs, throwing long passes or making long runs.

Curtis McClinton on John Hadl

John Hadl was mystical. Our sophomore year, John did some things that were just incredible. He returned an interception 98 yards against TCU, had a 94-yard punt against Oklahoma, and a 97-yard kickoff return against Syracuse. His leadership and inspiration were very important to our whole team. When we played TCU, I remember Jack Spikes running, and John put a hit on him that forced him to fumble—we got the ball. He was really an inspiring leader—bright, intelligent—and he knew how to use his assets. He worked me in every way, as a receiver, runner, blocker. And he always had a bite about him, and that bite was excellent. He was a strong leader, and we respected him. He could do it with you and he could do it on his own.

When John and I were playing in the All-Star Shrine game in San Francisco after our senior season, the game was winding down but he continued to run me and throw me the ball. I said, "John, come on, we're winding it down, the game's almost over." And he said, "We've got to finish the game out, bring it to closure." He was probably one of the most tenacious, dogged winners I ever played with throughout my entire football career.

CHAPTER 4

Jack Mitchell— Winning with Enthusiasm

"Coming to the University of Kansas to coach was what I'd always wanted."
—Jack Mitchell

The Kansas football program was a shambles when he took it over, and it had hit hard times again when he was forced out. But in between, Jack Mitchell's teams thrilled KU football fans. With the likes of John Hadl, Curtis McClinton, Gale Sayers and many others, Mitchell almost always fielded a strong team. With the exception of a couple of seasons, the Jayhwks were a squad to be reckoned with by the other schools in the conference.

"It just takes a lot of hard work," Mitchell said of putting together a college football team. "I did have good players. Actually, our number-one priority was this: We've got to get the blue chippers in the state of Kansas. I don't care what the cost."

He got them.

Just three years after taking over the program, Mitchell guided the Jayhawks to a 7-2-1 record and the Big Eight title (which was later forfeited). The following year the team won the Bluebonnet Bowl, and for the next three seasons battled to the end of each season with a chance to either win the conference or go to a bowl game.

After winning just two games in 1965 and 1966, Mitchell was forced out as the Jayhawks head coach. But it was one of his final recruiting classes, the seniors in 1968, who were so instrumental in taking Kansas to the Orange Bowl.

"When we had those bad seasons, they were not the result of bad players," Mitchell said of the 1965-66 seasons. "I got involved in too many activities outside of football."

Jack Mitchell

All my life, my ambition was to go to KU. I thought that that's where you died and went to heaven, in Lawrence, Kansas. But as it worked out, I didn't make it there as a player. When I came back from the service, it just didn't work out. They were recruiting me heavily, but they had so much more to offer, it seemed, at Oklahoma. But I still had that craving, that desire for KU. When I got into coaching, I figured that the KU coaching job was a diamond in the rough. They weren't doing too well, and I couldn't understand why when they were up there next to Kansas City, why in the hell they couldn't get the boys, and why they couldn't have a football team. I just thought it was a great opportunity. In the meantime, I got my first head coaching job at Wichita State. I did real well there and got an opportunity to go to Arkansas as head coach. I went down to the University of Arkansas and did well there, too. It was just a wonderful school, and I figured that I would be there the rest of my life. At that time, KU had just lost about 40 games in four or five years. You can imagine what their program was like. Chuck Mather was the head coach, and they were at the bottom of the barrel. Kansas didn't have anything there to attract a coach.

So they came down to see me, and there it was, my life's ambition right in front of me. I didn't tell them how much I wanted to come, of course. I'd have paid them, but they didn't know that. I would never have left Arkansas for any place but KU. And I told Arkansas when I was there and they gave me a contract stating that if they ever did offer me the opportunity, that I'd go to KU. No other place. Oklahoma? No, I'd stay right there. But, if KU offered me a job, that's what I'd always wanted to do. And it happened.

The chancellor was Franklin Murphy, and what a great guy he was. I had about 30 things that we needed to have to win. When I went up there, I held all the marbles, and I said to Franklin Murphy: "Chancellor, I have a list here I want you to look at." They had a big party for me when I came up to visit—not to take the job, but just to visit. Franklin Murphy was just a little ole guy. He only weighed about 145 pounds and was about five foot nine inches. I had already shown the list to the athletic director, who said it was all right with him, but I needed to show it to the chancellor. That list had a lot of things on it, that's for sure. But, I just put it down in black and white what I needed to win. So, I kept talking with the chancellor and he said, "You keep talking about a list, where is that list?" I said it's right here. "Oh my God," he said, "you have 30 things written down here." I said yeah, I want you to look at all of them. And the list had nothing to do with money. I knew they weren't going to pay me what I wanted. I wasn't concerned about that. It was things we need to win and the assistant coaches situation. I had to have a good spot for them and had to have plenty of them. He looked at the list and said: "Jack, I don't know what it takes to win. You're supposed to know. Sure, if that's what it takes to win and the athletic director has looked at it and okayed it, then sure." I asked him if he would mind signing his signature right here on it? Would he do that? And, he signed it. You can't believe the things I had on that list. In three years we won the Big Eight Championship.

Curtis McClinton

I was a snotty-nosed kid from Wichita, Kansas. I didn't know anything but practicing football, running track and studying. I visited my fraternity, and every now and then, I'd have a date. I didn't know anything about politics. As a matter of fact, I read things now that I didn't even know were happening at the time. When you talk about some of these things, I'm not altogether sure that as a student I was really aware of it. I know what our record was each year, and I know we played some good ball clubs.

We showed that Coach Mitchell had recruited some strong, talented guys.

Bobby Douglas

Jack Mitchell, in my opinion, was as good a recruiter as there was in the country. If you know Jack Mitchell, he has one of the great personalities of all time. He's just a wonderful guy, a good person and was a great salesman. Of all the coaches I have ever seen recruit or known personally, he's right there at the top, being able to recruit with his personality and demeanor. I really did like Jack, and that was a big part of why I went to KU. From a coaching standpoint, Jack was a good football coach. Things were changing, and I think he probably needed to upgrade his coaching staff. I think KU needed to upgrade their football program in general at that point. That's when the southern schools started "redshirting," although I think KU redshirted some. A lot of things were happening in college football, mainly in the south, at that time. I think Jack should have looked at some of that, and I think that maybe he would have. But he didn't really get along with Wade Stinson (KU's athletic director at the time) that well from what I could see, and of course, from what I've heard. There are probably a lot of reasons why he shouldn't have lost his job then, but I think because of Stinson he did lose it.

Jack Mitchell

I wasn't that good of a recruiter. It just takes a lot of hard work. I did have good players. Actually, our number-one priority was this: We had to get the blue chippers in the state of Kansas. I don't care what the cost, I don't care what you've got to do, I don't care what it is, but nobody leaves the state of Kansas. That was a priority when I got the job and hired the coaches. I had five coaches. I had four of them cover each corner of the state, and they'd find the prospects. And I had it figured—this wasn't hard—it was pretty well known, that out of so many million people, there are so many flute players, there are so many basketball players—I'm talking about blue chippers. With the population of Kansas at that time, I figured we had 22-23 blue-chip football players. And, out of those, some of their grades will fall. Some of them will get in trouble. You can't get them all, but you probably can come up with 13-14 who make a nucleus of the best players in the state, if you get them. Our priority was to never lose a Kansas boy. We could not lose one to K-State. Of course, K-State wasn't anything then, so that wasn't really a problem. And we did it; we controlled the state. We never did lose a single player. I don't remember a single player leaving the state of Kansas and going to another college in the 10 years that I was there.

Curtis McClinton

Coach Mitchell is a coach I've always admired since I was a kid at Wichita, because he coached at Wichita State. I always remember Coach Mitchell for his innovativeness. I used to go out to the games and watch Wichita play, and I fell in love with the Wichita program. When Jack left Wichita and went to Arkansas, I almost followed him. Of course, when he left Arkansas and came to KU, it really didn't surprise me, because we all loved Kansas. And what he pulled together was the best crop of

Kansas players ever up to that time. Guys like John Hadl and I and a whole group of other great guys who came together to play for Kansas.

John Hadl

Jack was probably the greatest recruiter in the history of recruiting—period. He had a way about him, especially in those days. Jack had the gift of gab and was a good-looking guy. The parents loved him, he had a lot of enthusiasm and made you believe that everything was going to happen, that the team was going to be great in a short period of time. And actually, as it turned out, pretty much everything he said would happen did happen. He had a good staff of people. He recruited a great freshman class that first year of Kansas kids, as well as some Texas kids, and he just did a great job. That's what it was all about at that time.

Jack Mitchell on the Sky Blue Uniforms

When I went to KU, they were wearing red jerseys. Everybody was wearing red—Nebraska, Oklahoma, Iowa State. I decided the first thing I was going to do was to get rid of those goddamn red jerseys. I remember asking, "What in the hell are the colors at KU?" When I found out they were blue and red, I remember thinking, "Hell, I didn't know that." I thought it was red and something else. Well, the sky blue hit me good, because when I played for OU and we played North Carolina in the Sugar Bowl, they had blue uniforms and I thought those were the prettiest uniforms I ever saw in my life. I never did forget them. When I found KU's colors were blue, the first thing I did was put sky blue pants on the team. We had sky blue jerseys, sky blue helmets and sky blue pants.

Bert Coan

Coach Mitchell was funny in a lot of ways, and he was also kind of temperamental. He would go off the handle, kind of lose it sometimes during the game. Boy, I think he was so nervous sometimes he would lose control. I think the assistant coaches had to calm him down a little bit, or try to. I think he just wanted to win so bad. I've seen him blow his top, like he was going crazy at times. I don't know if it was an act or not—it was probably more that than anything else. He was real volatile, but a real decent, nice person, and a bit of a jokester. He had a lot of playfulness about him.

There was this incident at halftime where he went crazy. That was when I was a red shirt—the 1959 season—so I wasn't playing. In those days, he had a blackboard he drew plays and stuff on, and he got mad, threw a fit and started pounding that blackboard. He beat that blackboard down to the floor and kicked it, but finally it looked like he regained control of himself. One of the assistant coaches came over and set the blackboard back up. And then he had another fit and pounded it down again. He took the blackboard out twice, just beat it to smithereens in front of everybody. I don't know if it fired anybody up or not. Of course, after the game, he'd call a player up and apologize for the way he jumped on them during a game. I don't know if there was some psychological motive to it or not. He never really jumped on me, but he did run me off a couple times.

Don Fambrough

Jack was a great recruiter—that was his main thing. He loved to recruit and he loved to be with people. He could go out every night and be with a group of people. I think the biggest mistake, and we've made a lot of them, but one of the biggest mistakes that they ever made was not making Jack athletic director. I think that's what he really wanted to be there at the end. He would have loved to have been athletic director. And if they would have done that, we would not have been so far behind with our facilities and so forth, because Jack was able to go out and raise money. He could talk people into anything. So his main asset was his ability to recruit, to raise money. Every Monday night we had a quarterback club meeting— we used to laugh about this—and hell, we could get beat

Jack Mitchell (left) and his top assistant coach, Don Fambrough, discuss game strategy. *University of Kansas Archives*

35 to nothing and Jack would go before that group on Monday night and before the program was over he'd have everyone thinking we won the football game. I tell you he was just super on his feet. He was just as good a coach, and he had great ability to hire good assistant coaches.

Bobby Skahan

One of the weirder things—or at least different—that happened while I was playing at Kansas was that we had red helmets in 1965. It surprised me and everybody else. I don't remember whose idea it was, I think the sports information director at the time. He thought it would be good to have red helmets. I wasn't very happy about it, and most of the other players weren't very happy about it, either. They almost looked like Oklahoma's helmet, red with a white KU logo on the side.

John Hadl

Jack would chew your ass out, or he would give you a big speech. One time, at the half, we were ahead but we weren't playing very well. He started yelling and screaming, trying to get us fired up. He turned around and slugged the chalkboard. I saw him wince a little, then he said, "Let's go!" Everyone got up and left, but I stopped and looked at him. He was bent over grabbing his wrist— there was a 2x4 behind the chalkboard. He cracked his wrist and he hid it until we got out the door.

Jack Mitchell

We had a new chancellor come in after Franklin Murphy went to UCLA. With the new president, all the things I needed to run the program disappeared. They'd given me a lifetime contract, and I knew there was a little resentment because there wasn't a professor on campus who had a lifetime contract. And, that's the worst thing that can happen—you get a little resentment. I think that contract was a bad thing when they did that. Of course, at the time I thought it was a great, and I accepted it. But I think overall it hurt me. Then, things kind of got a little bit worse. It just wasn't the same. Finally, it just came down to the point where I was just tickled to death to get out of it because everything had changed so much. It got to the point that all I was doing was fighting the administration. I thought they were selfish and not understanding—I could have been more patient with them and worked it out. So, I'm as much to blame as they were. I got involved in other activities, and that was my fault.

Bobby Skahan

I thought it was really sad—Coach Mitchell shouldn't have been fired. Jack should've been the athletic director. He should've just been moved to that position. There was a squabble between him and the current director, they didn't see eye to eye, and Jack would've been a great AD. He was great with people and would have helped with recruiting for all sports. For some reason, they didn't like Jack. There was always that animosity and strife.

CHAPTER 5

Pepper Rodgers— Witty and Fun

"There are too many disappointing things in life that are going to happen to you for you to not run a [football] program where it is fun to play."

—Pepper Rodgers

When Pepper Rodgers took over the football program at the University of Kansas following the 1966 season, the team was coming off one of its worst seasons ever—a record of 2-7-1—and the prospect of turning things around didn't look good. That didn't seem to bother Pepper, who had a way of making the best out of difficult situations.

"That was a fun time for me," Rodgers said of his stint as KU's coach. "But life has always been fun for me." It was also a fun time for KU fans when Pepper walked the sidelines at Memorial Stadium.

After guiding the Jayhawks to a 5-5 record and a surprising second-place finish in the Big Eight in 1967, Rodgers led KU to a 9-1 record in 1968 and a share of the Big Eight crown. The big prize was a berth in the Orange Bowl, where the Jayhawks lost a real heartbreaker to Penn State, 15-14. Kansas's fortunes did a complete reversal the following season, however, as KU won only one game. The team rebounded a bit in 1970, finishing with a mark of 5-6. Rodgers left Mount Oread after that, taking the head coaching position at UCLA. His time at KU, though short, has always brought a smile to the KU fans who remember his witty sense of humor and excellent coaching skills.

Pepper Rodgers on Coming to KU

I was assistant coach at UCLA. I'd been there for two years. They called me from KU and asked me to come back for an interview. I came back for an interview, went back to the hotel room, and then they came over and offered me the job—so there I was.

First of all, they don't hire coaches from the outside when a team has a good year. Obviously, I was thrilled to be a head coach. I had been an assistant coach for seven years and I was a young guy. It was a thrill for me. I feel very close to Kansas. It's like your first baby or your first love. KU has always had a special place for me in my heart.

Bobby Douglas

When I first met Pepper, I liked him. He's a very enthusiastic guy, a very positive kind of a person. He took control of things, and I usually got along with him very well. I was in a situation where I was kind of being challenged by the coaches, because I was a sophomore who had started six or seven games, but didn't do much. Not so much because it was me, it was just the whole situation with the team. Football is a team sport, and no matter what anyone says, the team has to be a good team. No player, today or at any other time in football, can do it on his own.

When Pepper and his staff came to KU, I was told "You are going to have to win the job." But they were very positive about it, and it worked out fine. Pepper was one of those guys who really understood what he wanted to do as a football coach. He certainly didn't seem like an assistant coach when he came in there. I think he was very organized in the way he handled the football situation and the discipline of the players. We had a very tough off-season program. Extremely tough. They wanted to get the players ready to play football. Pepper was an excellent football coach, there's no doubt about that.

Pepper Rodgers

My father, Franklin Rodgers, was one of the greatest recruiters in all the world and he helped us get a lot of players out of Atlanta. Dad didn't have much to do with the team, but he knew all the high school principals. So he was signing up two guys who were coming KU. One of the assistant coaches who was with him down there wanted to get back, so my daddy asked this kid to sign before the next morning, which was when he legally allowed to sign. He signed, gave them to the coach, and the coach went on home. The next day the K-State coach (Vince Gibson) calls the kid, and the kid tells him he'd signed with Mr. Rodgers and KU last night. We signed three kids. If I'd gotten a call letting me know what was going on, I'd have torn up the letters. Instead of that, Vince turns us in. That's what it was about. We signed the guys the night before we were supposed to, and they took 15 scholarships from us.

David Jaynes

Sure, I wanted to play for Pepper. When you're being recruited, a big part of why you go to a certain place is for the football staff that recruits you, and the head coach. It was a disappointment. Pepper called me into his office and one the things he said to me was, "I've coached Steve Spurier, and he was an All-American and won the Heisman trophy. I've coached Gary Beban, and he was an All-American who won the Heisman trophy. You have the potential to be as good as either one of those guys." I knew he was telling me that to get me thinking that I could do something at KU. He left with real positive feelings and half the staff didn't go with him.

Peace

It was the worst beating a Pepper Rodgers KU team took, and it was at the hands of the hated Missouri Tigers. The 1969 season had been disastorous for the

Jayhawks—they lost to K-State for the first time in 15 years, at home—lost a controversial game at Nebraska and by three points each to Oklahoma State and Colorado. When the Tigers rolled into Memorial Stadium for the season's final game, Kansas was 1-8 and MU was 8-1. And once the game started, the Tigers scored seemingly at will, and they were not bashful about running up the score.

The final tally was Missouri 69, Kansas 21.

Later in the year at a Big Eight meeting, Pepper joked about the game, how in the fourth quarter he had flashed Dan Devine, Missouri's coach, the peace sign, but had received only half of it back. In other words, Devine flipped off Pepper. It's been a famous story for the past 35 years.

"It was only a joke," Rodgers said of the "peace sign" incident. "I made that up—I was joking. I mean, Dan was just so stiff. There's no way he would have ever done that. The fact is it was a joke. We got our asses beat, and I simply made up a funny thing."

Pepper Rodgers

In football, you really find out if you can coach when you go into a place and you take your predecessor's players and win. Three years later, you find out if you can recruit. There's a difference.

We had a system and we believed in the system. I'd been an assistant coach at UCLA. We had been to the Rose Bowl and had two great football teams with the system that I took back with me to Kansas. This featured a quarterback who could run with a ball…. it was basically a single wing from a T-formation. We were very fortunate to have Bobby Douglas there at the time, who hadn't really had much success until then. The offense really suited for him. That really made it good. We just stayed with the system and continued to believe in what we were doing.

In 1968, John Riggins became a sophomore, which obviously upgraded the team immensely. I went out and not only recruited constantly, but we recruited from the basketball team. We recruited guys off the track team who could run fast and played them at wide receivers. We helped ourselves by bringing in people from other sports. I had a young coaching staff, and Don Fambrough was a tremendous help to me. He knew the school, he knew the players and he knew a lot about the KU tradition.

Number 100

The 1969 football season marked the 100th anniversary of college football. To commemorate the celebration, many of the nation's top football programs added a "100" decal to their helmets. It was a standardized logo—a football-shaped oval with "100" in the middle. Some teams wore them on the side of their helmets, others on the front.

Kansas opted not to wear the logo. Instead, the media office petitioned the NCAA and asked special permission for one player to wear the number 100 on his jersey—for the 1969 season only—as a way for the school to commemorate the anniversary. The NCAA agreed.

KU punter/place kicker Bill Bell was selected, and throughout the '69 season, he wore jersey number 100, the only time that has been permitted in KU football history.

"I wasn't in charge of numbers," Rodgers recalled of Bell's jersey number. "I think that was a media relations thing. I remember Bell in the Orange Bowl, though. At one point he thought we were going to punt, but we

During the 1969 season, Kansas kicker Bill Bell wore jersey number 100. *University of Kansas Archives*

kicked, and he had the wrong shoe on. That's all I remember."

Pepper Rodgers

It's hard to win nine or 10 games at Kansas. It's hard. It's a basketball school. The state doesn't have that many football players, and when you are lucky enough to get guys like John Riggins, that's a real exception to the rule. So consequently, you have to fight like hell to stay above water. It's just tough. Jack Mitchell left us some really good players and we were really fortunate to have those players.

Don Fambrough

We had that great team in 1968, we played in the Orange Bowl, and the next year we went from 9-2 to 1-9, Following the 1970 season, Pepper got an opportunity to go to UCLA. Now this is the type of person Pepper was. He comes into my office, closes the door and sits down. He said, "Don, I'm going to accept a job at UCLA and I'm going to recommend that they appoint you as head football coach." Wade Stinson was athletic director. I never will forget the day I was sitting in my office and I was thinking, "Well, Pepper's going to UCLA. Boy, I don't want to go to UCLA. I don't want to go to California. I want to stay here.' Then Wade stuck his head in the door and he said, "Don, you're going to be the next head football coach at the University of Kansas." That's all he said and he left. He didn't ask me whether I wanted the job or not, he just said I was going to be the next head football coach.

Well, getting back to Pepper, that was my first opportunity at being a head football coach and we had a tremendous staff there. We had John Cooper. We had Terry Donahue. We had people like that. We had Charlie McCuller. And so Pepper called me in his office after I'd been announced as head football coach and he said, "Don, I want to divide the staff up. I'm going to take part of them with me, but I want to leave some with you." And he left the better coaches with me. He left Larry Travis with me. He left John Cooper with me. He left Charlie McCuller with me. That's the type of person he was, because he wanted me to succeed knowing that was my first job as a head football coach. I don't know very many football coaches who would have done that. But that was Pepper. We were very close and are still very close.

Pepper Rodgers

So we beat Nebraska twice. The third time—1969—we should have beat them up there. My point is that this team beat Nebraska twice, and that's pretty good. We went to the Orange Bowl and that's damn good. It's hard to go to the Orange Bowl in the Big Eight. Particularly, it's hard at Kansas, because there aren't enough football players in Kansas. We were fortunate to get some great Kansas players, and we filled in with some great players from out of state. We were really fortunate also because a lot of southern schools weren't recruiting black athletes, so we were able to help ourselves in that way, too.

Missouri, of course, was a big game for Kansas at that time, and I assume it still is. We beat them twice, they beat us twice. The fact is that the two times we beat them, they had very good football teams. When they beat us, we weren't that good. The rivalry between those two schools is the same as between Georgia and Georgia Tech…it's a great rivalry. Missouri at that time was really good. We went to the Orange Bowl one year, they went the next year.

Pepper gets a kiss from the Orange Bowl Queen before the game with Penn State in the 1969 Orange Bowl. Penn State defeated the Jayhawks, 15-14. *University of Kansas Archives*

CHAPTER 6

Rivalries— How to Twist a Tiger's Tail

"We'll put Missouri's Tiger so far in the tank they'll never come out."
—KU's Chancellor, 1960s

Most schools have one big rival, an opposing school that triggers their anger and makes the alumni sick. An opponent so repulsive, so hated, the mere thought of losing to them is unfathomable. A rivalry born in bitterness, bathed in blood. One rival.

But KU has two.

The Missouri Tigers have always been the Jayhawks' traditional rival, a mutual loathing that dates to the Civil War. The first football game between the two schools took place in 1891, and the series has been as even as it has been ill-tempered. The overwhelming joy felt by Jayhawk football fans when KU defeats Missouri is shared by the players, maybe more so, so strong is the sense of competition between the two schools.

Kansas's other top rival is K-State, a rivalry born more out of the Wildcats dislike for KU than any other factor. The series was completely dominated by KU in the 20th Century, but football fortunes have not been kind to Kansas the past decade when they play K-State. The Jayhawks last defeated the Wildcats in 1992—but there is hope. Hope and spirit are always around in rivalry games—and hatred.

Nolan Cromwell on the K-State Rivalry

When I was in school, I think for the student body, the KU–K-State rivalry was the biggest. We were both fairly even football teams as far as being athletically matched. It was really a great rivalry. I think for the alumni (the older alums), the KU/Missouri game was the most important. I think a lot of the alumni from both schools have settled in the Kansas City area. There's a lot of competition and pride there. Vince Gibson was the coach at K-State at the time and they had their Purple Pride slogan. I'll never forget my senior year, having my knee injury and not getting to play in the Missouri game. It was at Columbia. They really honored me by having me come out and kind of saluted me prior to the game. I kind of hobbled out on the field and shook hands with a lot of their players. It really meant a lot to me, that Missouri was able to do that and honor me in that fashion. And then we just killed them in the game. I think it was 41 to 14.

Don Fambrough on Missouri

I get all fired up when we play Missouri. Even though sometimes now we don't play them the last game like we always did, it's still to me a two-season deal. It's everybody else and then Missouri. And people have often said, why do you dislike Missouri so much? And I have to say, "It's just because they're so easy to dislike."

Moran Norris, the Rivalries

The KU–K-State game was supposed to be a big game, but really, KU and Missouri is a bigger rivalry match up. You know how it used to be that the raiders from Missouri came to Kansas and raped all the women? Burn the town? or something like that—the coaches and other people always used to bring it up. That game was a tradition for us—a big game. It was something that you kind of take personally. I remember when we went to Columbia to play there, their fans would throw bottles, junk, all kinds of stuff at us.

Otto Schnellbacher, the Rivalries

Phog Allen and George Sauer hated Missouri with a passion. It was always a very crucial ballgame. The "Antlers" were there just like they are now. All the

Moran Norris. *KUAC Media Relations*

years I was in school, we never spent the night in Columbia. After the game, we went back to the hotel, got showered and cleaned up. We would just go down to the locker room, pick up our stuff and go to the hotel. We'd all get in four or five rooms, take our showers, get dressed and leave. And we always stayed somewhere 40 to 50 miles outside of Columbia.

K-State has never been what I consider a rivalry game. Missouri has always been the top competition, the team I've wanted to beat. K-State now is beginning to get my attention. I'd like to beat them, because so many of their alumni have come out of the woodwork. They are not very gracious winners and that's beginning to upset me a little bit. Other than that, they've never been the great rivalry that Missouri was. I always felt in my day, that Nebraska was the one we had to take care of. And, of course, Oklahoma under Bud Wilkinson.

Emmett Edwards on Beating Missouri in 1973

We threw the ball around a lot in 1973. We lost a close one to Nebraska—we played three real close games that season. The Tennessee game (we lost 28-27) gave us a hint that we were headed in the right direction, and sort of set the tone for what was to come. We needed the Missouri game to get a bowl bid. It was a cloudy, chilly day in Lawrence, and it ended up being a good game—a lot was riding on the outcome, at least for us. It was close, but I think we wanted to win more than Mizzou. We found ourselves in a position where we had just a little time left in the game to go a long way, and that's what we did. We put that winning drive together, gained

Emmett Edwards. *University of Kansas Archives*

momentum, and scored the winning touchdown right at the end.

Harrison Hill on KU's Rivalries

I dislike them both so much. K-State was a little different for me, being from Wichita and having friends who went to K-State. When they started getting good in the '90s, I saw so many people in the Kansas area jump on that bandwagon. It was hard when they were beating us because I would go home to Wichita and all I would hear about was K-State football. It made me sick because there was nothing more I wanted than to beat K-State. I hate Missouri and Coach Fambrough would probably hate me for saying this, but I'd rather beat K-State than Missouri just because of the in-state rivalry, just because they think they're better than us. They think they have the top Western Kansas boys. There's nothing worse for me then going to Manhattan and losing to K-State. I mean, the look of Manhattan, the smell of Manhattan, the fans…I just get sick to my stomach thinking about it. Not just because we got our butts kicked, but because I just dislike so many things about them. My dad wouldn't even go to the K-State games because he was the same way; he hated them, too.

I didn't even know how much of a rival Missouri was until I came here. To be honest, I didn't even feel it until we were playing at Missouri in 1998. When the offense came off the field I was getting hit with oranges and batteries. The student section was throwing stuff at us. I've never seen a more classless bunch in all of college football and that's what spurred my dislike for Missouri. It was really the fans and how classless they were and how no one

Harrison Hill. *KUAC Media Relations*

controlled the place. The fans could do whatever they wanted and it was just like a zoo in there.

By far, my favorite game of my career was 1999 Missouri at home. The night before in the hotel, John Hadl and Coach Fambrough were in the hotel. They gave speeches about what they felt about Missouri and how important this game was to KU alumni and fans. We went out the next day and beat Mizzou 21-0. That was probably the happiest I ever was in college, and not only because we played well. After we scored a touchdown, Fambrough was on the sidelines with the biggest grin I'd ever seen on his face, pumping his fist—I loved seeing how much it meant to him. I thought it was so great to win for somebody like him, and I also know that it means so much to so many people. That's why I love being at KU. Fambrough wore that jersey, he coached against Missouri, and he wanted nothing more than to beat them. It put a smile on his face. It was awesome. By far, that was the best game of my life. We hated Missouri, we shut them out and having Gale Sayers and others give us speeches before the games, and then to go out and win it for them was awesome for me.

David Jaynes on Beating Missouri in 1973

For the final touchdown play against Missouri in 1973, there were three of us there, Coach Fambrough, Coach McCuller and me. We called time out, went to the sidelines and started talking. We called the play, and Delvin Williams was going to run a flat pattern. We believed they were going to be in man to man and that Delvin would be one on one with the outside linebacker. We thought that we could get the ball to him and he could at least get the first down from the pass. When the ball was snapped, I dropped back and looked to the spot where Delvin was going to be. He was out there, but the linebacker had sprinted out there, and there was no way I would get the ball to him or that he would get the first down. I had no choice but to go to the next guy, Emmett Edwards. His man was all over him, but Emmett made a great catch. I really had no choice, because when the ball was snapped, I really thought I was going to throw it to Delvin.

Marlin Blakeney on K-State

It sucked that we didn't beat K-State again after 1992. In 1993, we lost in Manhattan, I think the score was 10-9—a frustrating game. We had a couple calls that didn't go our way. They had a late touchdown that gave them the lead and we couldn't catch them. That one hurt.

Overall, the K-State and Missouri games are just bigger games. Those are games that you feel like you've got to win, and the pressure is enormous. We beat Mizzou all but one year that I was there. The Tony Sands game in 1991 was awesome when he broke the record for most rushing yards in a game. You could always tell Missouri wanted to win and they played hard, but they kind of played dirty, like you'd make a tackle and get punched in the pile or they'd grab your facemask and rub it in—something like that. I made one play and the referee was on the Missouri sideline and I was getting kicked—kicked in the ribs. I think Steve Harvey came in and cleaned everything out. He picked me up and said let's go.

Marlin Blakeney. *KUAC Media Relations*

Bobby Douglas on K-State

My dad played at K-State. I was born in Manhattan, and I went to K-State games. They recruited me. I just never thought about it because they weren't good enough. You always want to play in a good program. KU was borderline, maybe. Let's face it, Kansas was 6 and 4 my senior year in high school, but they were competitive. And, in those days, you don't know as much as high school kids know today. You know about the school, but you don't really follow them for 20 years like you do now. Everything is on ESPN. Kansas basketball, North Carolina basketball and Kentucky. In those days, you knew about a few things. OU was big-time football, and they offered me a scholarship, but Bud Wilkinson had quit, I think, two years before that.

Spencer Bonner on the Rivalries

Actually, you kind of feel the two rivalries—Missouri and K-State—the first year that you're at KU. When I came to Kansas, I had never even heard of K-State, being from Chicago. I never knew anybody who even knew anybody who went to K-State. When I got here, the K-State rivalry was huge. That was 1991 and KU lost to K-State. You could see it in the guys when they came back how upset they were compared to any other game that we had lost that season. After that game, people were really upset for the whole week. From that point on, you could really tell that that game was huge.

John Hadl on the 1960 Missouri Game

Bert Coan was one of the most highly recruited players in the country that year. He ended up at TCU and he didn't like it that well after he got there. Somehow he and Bud Adams got connected. Bud gave him a ride from the Chicago all-star game down to Dallas and dropped him. In those days there was nothing wrong with that, he didn't do anything but give him a ride. But there were some Missouri alumni on that flight, and they called the Missouri coach and that's what triggered that whole thing. The ironic thing was that it was a couple years later, before they turned Bert in. We were leading the conference in 1960, beating off everybody and ranked pretty well in the country. All of a sudden at the Missouri game we got hit with it. Missouri was number one and we were fourth or fifth. Missouri was undefeated. They made us forfeit the games from earlier in the year so our record was not as good as it really was. Bert played against Missouri and he was Back of the Week for the Nation that week.

Missouri was the biggest game of the year. It still is just because of the bitter rivalry. I think we're one game up on them after more than 100 years of playing football. They really hate us and we really despise them. There are no questions about that.

Jack Mitchell on Beating Missouri in 1960

I got a call from Bud Adams, who owns the Tennessee Titans, which used to be the Houston Oilers. He was a KU alumni. All the Adamses are KU alumni. We were talking and I told him we needed all the help we could get. I needed to get some good players and I needed to get someone from out of state. Could he help me? He said sure, and he helped me with several players from down there. Then he called me and told me he had a boy working for him and that the boy was a great football prospect. He was at TCU, but he wasn't real happy there because they told him he could go out for track and he was not satisfied with the way they were handling it. His spring football practice was at the same time as track. He was the fastest high school kid in the world at that time—I'm talking about the whole world. He had a record of 9.5 or something in the 100-yard dash. That's how fast that guy was. He was six foot four and weighed 220. You can imagine what kind of a player he was.

Bud was on his way to the airport to go to the Chicago All-Star game. I think he had a chauffeur and he stopped to get gas. The guy who filled them up was Bert Coan. Bud said he was going to Chicago to the All-Star game, and Bert said something like that would sure be great. Bud asked if he would like to go, and Bert went with him. As I understand it, TCU had a board of regents man on the airplane with Bud and they took him to the ball game. They said that was illegal because alumni can't take someone on a big trip like that. But it was before we [KU] even got involved in it. We didn't even know about him then. Was it illegal? Well, it might be and it might not be. Regardless, it ended up—after the fact—that Bert was ruled ineligible.

But Coan was declared okay by the NCAA. Those games were not forfeited by the NCAA. The Big Eight conference had several votes on the deal and they voted him ineligible for those three games in 1960. After Bud Wilkinson died, I asked his first wife, Mary, why Bud didn't vote for us. Hell, I played for the man! She said, "Jack,

I feel sick about it myself. But picture Bud. He's got Darryl Royal on one side of him in Texas and he's got you up here in Kansas. He was just fighting to keep his program together." I said I didn't see how I could bother him any. We were a threat to him, no question about it, because we were going real good, but I was one of players.

About the Missouri game in 1960, we just went over there and beat their ass. We had a better team. That was one of the greatest football teams in the history of KU. Would we have won the game without Bert Coan? Hell, yes, we would have won the game without him. Missouri didn't make a first down until the third quarter. We just kicked the shit out of them. It wasn't even a close ballgame. They were undefeated, but they hadn't played anybody.

Curtis McClinton on the Border War

Kansas and Missouri—it's tradition. If you join a family, and there's a family rival, you've got one side of the family and the other. That whole thing, Kansas-Missouri, goes back to the border war. Goes back to John Brown, to the free state/slave state. The last state to free the slaves was Missouri. It goes back to that whole situation. The chancellor of MU is an African American who is 43-44 years old and KU Chancellor Hemingway has his Ph.D. in African American studies. That was such a note of importance in our history and our society that you get a great scholar like Dr. Hemingway, a great man, that focused his life learning. His ability to collaborate, assimilate and gather knowledge on an international, universal basis to codify his supreme and empirical knowledge on African American studies.

Ray Evans on the Missouri Game in 1981

In 1981, we were ahead of Missouri 5-3 and Roger Foote intercepted a pass and ran it in for a touchdown to make the score 12-3. We then had the one nice drive of the day, and Garfield Taylor scored to make it 19-3, and there were like four minutes to go and the crowd started edging out to the sidelines and Mizzou scored right at the tail end of the game.

With about a minute to go, the fans—the students, I guess—went crazy and rushed the field, tore down the goalpost in the south end of the stadium, and would have torn down the other goalposts if they hadn't been stopped. The officials gave KU 45 to 60 yards of penalties, which basically put the ball almost into the end zone for Mizzou. They scored, got a two-point conversion, which made the score 19-11, and then recovered an onside kick. But that was it, and we won. And then the fans really went wild.

I remember at the end, going, "Well, shit." I don't even remember the last play of the game. Until the Mizzou game this year, I think that's the most sincere, unabashed joy I've seen at Memorial Stadium. We had a lot of guys from around there, from the state, on the team. And Coach Fambrough was such a true-blue, loyal Jayhawk, it was an easy team to like and identify with. It was sure fun.

Max Ediger on the Rivalries

Missouri and K-State were always big games to me. Missouri was always played at the end of the year. K-State was usually in the middle. The emotion of the crowd was always fun because regardless if it was a home game or an away game, there would be shouting and chants from the stands that I don't think has been duplicated since. I went to the last K-State game that we played—we got beat pretty bad—and there was no yelling in the stadium like there used to be. It's just not the same atmosphere. A lot of it may have to do with the fact that we really haven't been competitive with K-State. But it was just such a huge deal, a rivalry based on tradition and everything else.

I don't remember a lot of talk on the field between the teams. No more than any other game, anyway. I think the main thing that was different between K-State and KU was just the obvious rivalry. K-State, KU, and Missouri were all fighting over the same players. And you had a lot of players from the same high school, and one would go to Missouri, one to K-State, one to KU. Everybody knew a lot of the players. You played in the all-star games against each other.

Mike Norseth on Beating Missouri

My first Missouri game, in my junior year, was over there right before they fired their coach who had done so well. When we walked into the stadium they had signs everywhere saying to fire the coach—Warren Powers. The guy had taken them to a lot of bowl games, so we didn't understand all the backlash. As a team, we were like, "Okay, let's put the sword in him." We had no problem with that. The next year they brought in Woody Widenhofer, and he was supposed to be this defense genius. We were prepared to face some difficult schemes, but they played the most basic defense we had seen all year. That was a nice win for us as well. Anytime you can beat your rival in your last game it's nice.

Bill Whittemore on His Injury When Playing K-State in 2003

We were close to the goal line in the first quarter and ran the ball. I took a hit and felt a pop around my shoulder, my collar bone. I tried to get up and couldn't. Somebody pulled me up. You never know how bad something is going to be, but you hope it isn't anything serious. When they were looking at me on the sideline they couldn't find anything wrong it. But I couldn't lift my arm and I was in pain. We actually didn't find out what the problem was until we got back to Lawrence.

Not being able to play a complete game against K-State my senior year was one of the hardest things I had ever been through. I cried and cried in the locker room—I went in there after the injury. When the guys came in at the half, I couldn't show my face because I was devastated. And I didn't want the guys to see that I'd been crying. I wanted to play against K-State so bad—I really felt like we had a good chance in the game. Whatever they beat us by, they sure weren't that much better than we were. It was frustrating, one of the low points of my life.

Chip Hilleary on Losing to Missouri in 1992

It was extremely difficult for me because I had such a great following from my hometown, the fans and my family. I had probably 60 people at that game. Monte Cozzens, who played fullback for us, was also from my high school. Monte and I, that was our game. Who knows whether it was going to be our last game of four long years and four fun years to be at Missouri against a 100-year rival and have 60 people who have flown in from Columbus, Ohio, to watch us play. I got to play a little bit. But after that first drive—we scored on an option—I can remember coming off the field. I had, about two plays earlier, suffered a concussion from having my helmet slammed on the Astroturf. I don't remember the last two plays of that drive. The only thing I do remember is not knowing what a tiger formation was. When he signaled in the play, I couldn't get the signal. I can remember George White coming into the game, he was a tailback, and he said tiger formation, and there was also a 38 option. I didn't know what a tiger formation was. But I had 38 options so many times in my career that it was just automatic for me.

We scored, came off the field, and I could barely tell Lynn Bott, the trainer, what was going on. One of his rules was if you lost your memory, even temporarily, that he wouldn't let you go back in the game. Coach Mason had a hard time with it, but he agreed with Bott that if that were the case, I wouldn't go back in. I can remember Monte and I standing side by side at one end of the field. We had to watch the game. I can remember Preston and Thomas—they tried both of them at quarterback and we just couldn't do anything as an offense. It was heartbreaking.

The best feeling of my career was Thanksgiving Day a few weeks later, and I was sitting at home watching the watching the Oklahoma–Nebraska game with friends and family. I got a call from Glenn Mason after the game saying we were going to the Aloha Bowl. I would have one more chance to end my career with the Kansas Jayhawks on national television against Brigham Young. That was freaking me out. That was one of the best moments in my four-year career. It was almost a revival of being able to play again.

Bobby Skahan on the
1964 Missouri Game

Even though we lost to Missouri, we had a chance to go to a bowl game anyway. We beat Oklahoma State, K-State and Colorado. We should have beaten Nebraska, too. We played Missouri down there, and it was a cold day, like minus 7. We had them down 7-6 at half-time, but they just came out and kicked our rears in the second half.

The Sun Bowl was actually going to give us an invitation. Coach Mitchell said it was up to the guys on the team to decide if we wanted to go. We went into the room to vote, and a lot of different things came into play. Some of the guys wanted to go play pro ball, and they considered that. Ronnie Marsh was wanting to become a boxer, and he didn't want to play football anymore. We actually had several guys on that team who ended up playing pro ball. However, for some reason the seniors didn't want to go to the bowl game. Sad to say, we voted against it.

Harrison Hill on Playing Missouri

When you play Missouri in a packed house with KU fans and you beat them, it's such a rush—it's why you play football, it's why you go to college to a Big 12 school. You want to get out there in front of 50,000 fans and make a play so they scream. That's why you play the game. It's such an adrenaline rush to go out there, score a touchdown and look up at the crowd, seeing all those people screaming. It's addictive and it's a high. You live for that kind of stuff. When you walk out of the tunnel and it's a packed house, it's everything you wanted to do as a kid. It's there and you have to take advantage of it. I miss that, and every single player who's played the game misses that as much as anything, besides the comraderie. It's feeling the rush of all those fans and being in the spotlight. Nothing can compare to it, ever. You want to be a warrior.

Kelly Donohoe on the
KU–K-State Game in 1987

The low point, probably, in both KU's and K-States' football history is that Toilet Bowl game in the fall of 1987 (the game ended in a 17-17 tie). I don't know if KU and K-State were the worst teams in the country, but we were definitely at the bottom of the barrel. You just take pride and try to play your heart out because there are some things you can't control. You go into it knowing it's a big rivalry and you try to win anyway. After that, things got better for both programs. Coach Mason came on board at KU, and Bill Snyder was set to come on board for K-State, and things started picking up for both programs. But 1987 was definitely a tough year for us.

Chip Budde on the
KU–K-State Game in 1987

The Toilet Bowl. My favorite, all-time lead line in a sports story. It was in the *Topeka Capitol Journal*, I have no idea who wrote it, but it was "What happens when a resistible force meets a moveable object?" We went into the game with only one win. And in 1986 they beat us. It was my first year playing. The game was going back and forth, I'm surprised that anyone scored, really. And it came down to this: K-State was on our 20-yard line.

They were going to kick a field goal, and Marvin Maddox, who ended up playing on the National Championship basketball team later, made a fantastic play and we blocked the field goal. The game ended in a 17-17 tie.

Don Davis on Playing Missouri and K-State

I think the K-State games were definitely more intense than the Missouri games. The KU/Missouri games were there, but I felt like the older fans made more of the Missouri games than the players did. Still, it was always a good game for us. The one that really stands out in my mind is the game in 1992 when we lost to them before going to the Aloha Bowl. We lost the last three games of the season, and it was just awful.

Charlie Hoag on Playing Missouri

When I was a sophomore, we went over to Molbury, Missouri, worked out in sweatpants and t-shirts to prepare to play Missouri on Thanksgiving Day. On the day of the game, Thanksgiving, we went on into Columbia and there was a huge storm. It was very cold, probably around 12 degrees out. We showed up and had no cold weather gear, so Dean Nesmith, the trainer, went out to a sporting goods store and got some hand warmers. But by the second half it was so cold that everyone had gone home. I remember coming in at halftime and you know you're feeling sorry for yourself, you fumbled, your hands are frozen all the time, and by the time you got in the huddle and got a play called you couldn't feel anything. Anyway, we went in at halftime and there

Don Davis. *KUAC Media Relations*

was a KU band member standing by some sort of pot-belly heating unit, and he had pulled his horn off his lip after playing it. He tore a chunk out of his upper lip and his bottom lip was still frozen on the horn. He was getting it thawed out to get it off the metal. We were feeling sorry for ourselves, but after seeing that, I thought we weren't in as bad of shape as that kid was. But then nobody showed up for the second half and we fumbled our way through it. And it was too bad, because we were probably a better team than Missouri, although that was one competitive game.

Kerwin Bell

Through the years, I thought that playing K-State was a bigger deal. Maybe because we played them first, and they were in state. As the years have passed since I finished school, it was Missouri that was the biggest rival. Now, I totally understand it a little more. But K-State seemed bigger to me at the time, especially with the KU basketball team. I understand that Missouri was bad because of Quantrell's Raiders, and as I've gotten older, I really understand what that was all about.

CHAPTER 7

Magic Moments and Lost Dreams

"I think Nebraska was tough. When you walk on the field, you really respect what they have going there. Then I hear someone yell, 'Hey number 7, we're going knock your teeth out!' At that point you know you have to be ready to play."
—Mike Norseth

With the good times in KU's football history come the bad—or maybe it's the other way around. The Jayhawks have witnessed many great moments on the football field, and several not-so-good ones as well. From upsetting Oklahoma to making a once-in-a-lifetime play to getting pounded by Nebraska to suffering a freak injury to losing a heartbreaking game to pulling the prank, KU's teams and players have been through many different scenarios. Here's a few of those good, bad, funny—even a little sad—memories.

Nolan Cromwell on Beating Oklahoma in 1975

We'd never beaten Oklahoma. At that point in our season we were on a high. We were on a winning streak. Offensively, we were moving the football down the field. We were beginning to gel and play pretty well. It was exciting. We started the game and were able to move the football early, which kind of surprised us. All of a sudden it catches like fire that we can do this. We can move the ball up and down the field on these guys. We got a couple touchdowns early. They fumbled the ball about the first four times they had it in the second half. We ended up getting it and doing something with it. Then they went from running the wishbone offense to having to spread out more and throw. I think they threw four interceptions that game. Defensively we had eight or nine turnovers that game. We had a lot of opportunities to kick field goals or score points. It was very exciting in the fourth quarter when we knew we were going to win the game. Here was a school with such a long winning streak, and we were able to go in there and dominate. We really played very well. There just isn't a way to describe how excited our football team was at the end of that game.

Moran Norris on Nebraska

My junior year against Nebraska, we were so close in that game. I think we should have beaten

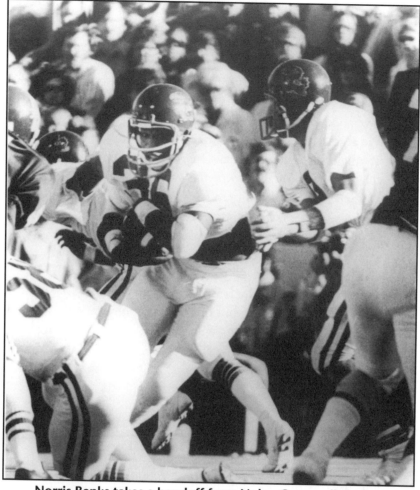

Norris Banks takes a handoff from Nolan Cromwell during the Jayhawks' 23-3 upset win over Oklahoma in 1975. *University of Kansas Archives*

them. That was a disappointment for the team because we played well and could have won. We lost it in the fourth quarter. The game was on TV, and I think we led most of the way. Personally, I had a pretty big game—I wanted to go out there and let Nebraska know we could play.

Marlin Blakeney on
Playing Nebraska in 1993

That would have turned our season around if we would have beaten Nebraska in 1993. We would have gone to a Bowl. Before that game, Coach Mason—he was a great speaker before games—said, "If we play well, we might have to make decisions, and if it comes down to whether to tie them or win the game, would you rather win and have a possibility to go to a Bowl game at the end of the season or would you rather take the tie? Which would you feel better about?" Everybody said the win. We wanted to win. So, the decision was made. When June Henley made that last touchdown we knew well in advance that we'd go for a two-point conversion. A lot of people don't know this, but on that two-point conversion Nebraska lined up wrong. We'd run that play in practice before, and we knew it would work. Coach Mason had done some research on how they set up to that formation. When the play works, the receiver is supposed to be wide open.

Everybody asked, "Why didn't June Henley get the ball? Why didn't he rush?" He had a great day, rushed for a lot of yards. He didn't run because he had a concussion and was on the sideline. They took him out—he didn't know where he was. I was on the sideline with him and asked him—he thought he was at home. The concussion happened on the touchdown play. He scored and something happened. Someone stepped on his head or he landed weird. So he came out. Coach Mason, I think he might have called a time out, and he asked everyone what they wanted to do again. We wanted to win, even though a kick conversion would have tied the game.

Anyway, Nebraska lined up wrong, so they had a player in the wrong place, but in the right place to stop the play and that's what killed it. Of course, we tried an onsides kick, and that failed—we lost, 21-20. Most of the guys on the team were down, knowing we could have tied it, but we weren't happy with that. You play hard and then you come down to that. We didn't beat Nebraska the whole time I was there, and I guess KU hasn't beaten them for a long, long time. That's the KU luck—Nebraska lines up wrong and ends up stopping our play.

Bobby Skahan on the 1964 Oklahoma Game

Oklahoma kicked off and Gale took the ball and returned it all the way. It was an incredible run. He just had that ability to accelerate. You'd think he was at full speed and then he'd just kick it in. He could weave left and right, and I don't know if he ever got touched. I remember him coming to the side and I went out to shake his hand, and he asked me what I thought about that run. We started laughing. He had that presence of mind on the field, had such great peripheral vision and the ability to turn it up a notch when he needed speed.

There were about 46 seconds left in the game and we were down on our 4-yard line. Oklahoma was ahead, 14-7. I came into the huddle and said, "If you guys block, we'll take this thing all the way." Everyone looked at me like I was nuts. That entire game had been a real defensive struggle—they beat us up the whole game. Gale's kickoff return was the only thing we'd done the entire game. In fact, I remember getting knocked out at one point when I ran an option and pitched the ball.

In that last series we commenced to throw the ball and run some draws. I think I threw eight or nine passes on the drive. There was a point where there was a big brawl in the middle of the field. Gale came in on a pass from the outside on the right sideline near our bench, and they took him out of bounds pretty hard. I think it was unnecessary roughness, and a brawl started for about five minutes. They broke it up and we marched down to the 20- or 30-yard line with about nine seconds left. We called a play where I pitched the ball to Dave Crandall. Dave reversed, then he lateralled back to me. I was supposed to throw the ball back to one of several potential receivers, but no one was really open, so I just took off. We threw off the defense by going from right to left.

I'll never forget that play because as I was at about the 14-yard line, Oklahoma's Lance Rentzel was chasing me. I saw him out of the corner of my eye. I knew that guy had speed, but I just kept going to the corner. I thought I could get in without going all the way to the flag, but he kept gaining on me. He was a big kid, and I thought he was going to take me out. I dove, hit the flag and got in. There wasn't any time left on the clock. We ran a reverse play for the two-point conversion to win the game, and everybody went nuts. It was an incredible experience, a once-in-a-lifetime finish.

Jack Mitchell on the 1964 Oklahoma Game

Gale Sayers ran the opening kickoff back, and Bobby Skahan, our quarterback, scored on the last play of the game—he just squeaked into the corner of the end zone after a long run. Then we went for the two-

KU quarterback Bobby Skahan (center) celebrates with
two of his offensive linemen after scoring a touchdown
on the final play of the 1964 KU-Oklahoma game. After
converting a two-point conversion, the Jayhawks won, 15-
14. *University of Kansas Archives*

point play with the double reverse to win, 15-14. That wasn't a tough decision, going for two against Oklahoma to win the game. Everybody would do it. Let me ask you this: What if you decide to tie the game and miss the extra point?

One of my best alumni friends always came down to the locker room after the game to congratulate me. He would have to leave his seat a little early to get down the stairs—he had one of those VIP seats at the 50-yard line—and we hadn't won the game with the two-point conversion until the time on the clock said 0:00. So when he left his seat, we were losing the game. He met me at the door of the locker room and said, "Gosh darn it, Jack, we'll get them next year. That Oklahoma played a hell of a game." I told him that we had won the game. "I know, Jack," he said, "it's too bad, don't let it upset you." I told him again that no, we won the game. He said, "I just had too much to drink...what?" Once more, I told him KU beat Oklahoma. "Oh my God!" he said, "We won the game!?" And then he fell over. Some of the players saw that and got a hell of a kick out of it.

Mike Norseth on Mike Gottfried

I really liked Coach Gottfried. He did a lot of good things. Certainly what he was doing offensively was equal to a lot of NFL teams at that time. I always had a lot of respect for him in that way. When you play for somebody, looking back now, it was almost a father-son relationship. Even though there was a quarterback coach, there was a lot of one-on-one with Coach Gottfried. Looking back he would probably do a few things differently or tweak some things. Overall though, he gave me a chance to play in the NFL, and it was a great opportunity.

Ray Evans on Nebraska and Oklahoma

Nebraska was always the toughest place to play, but not because of the crowd. Everyone thinks that, but there's more to it. They just play with so much confidence at home, would be so physical at their stadium—just so brutally physical.

Oklahoma was funny—we lost to them by one point Coach Moore's last year, and two years later we lost to them by two at home—we should've won both games. On the road the Sooners just kind of play well enough to win. Bud's last year, we were terrible and lost 17-16. I always felt like they were not into it. But the Nebraska kids would be prepared no matter what.

Charlie Hoag on the 1950 Colorado Game

One of my best games was against Colorado in 1950. Colorado came to Lawrence and had a 21-to-nothing lead. We hadn't done a thing for 30 minutes. They kicked off to start the second half and I was fortunate enough to run it back for a touchdown. And that started changing the momentum. Anyway, we scored, and I don't remember all the particulars, but we scored again the next time we got the ball, so now it was 21-14. We scored the third time, but missed the extra point, so it was 21-20. But we ended up scoring again and beating them 27-21. That was an exciting day, very exciting at Memorial Stadium. It was one of those games that, you know, the finish was just great.

Mike Norseth on the 1985 Season

My senior year we had a bunch of guys declared ineligible right before the season started, but it didn't seem like that big of a deal at that time. We were young and weren't expected to do a whole lot that year anyway. What the football department did was that they got an academic advisor who was supposed to make sure that everyone was eligible. That was the year the NCAA came out with the rule that all your hours had to be toward your degree. We had a great group of guys who stayed for the summer and took all the classes they were supposed to. There wasn't one person who didn't follow through and take all the classes they were supposed to according to the advisor. Then when we got to Hawaii for our first game, we had 11 guys ruled ineligible, and seven of them were starters, including our top two running backs. So we got hit with that right before our first game in Hawaii. When you look at that team and what we did, we would have been so much better with those other guys. We probably would have been one of the best teams in Kansas history. My understanding is that the Big 8 and the NCAA said that those guys were clear, but KU said no. You can be certain that this would never happen on the basketball level. Of course, you can't change things, but you still feel a little cheated.

David Jaynes on His First Game as the Starting Quarterback

The first game I ever started was against Nebraska at Lincoln. I don't remember what the score was,

Mike Norseth. *KUAC Media Relations*

but I do remember we didn't score a point. It was unbelievable. I was in awe, literally, as the game was going on—I couldn't believe the speed, the size, and the intensity of those guys. I just couldn't believe it. It was a rude awakening. I realized shortly after that they were just spectacular and not every team we were going to play was like that. They were incredible. I remember Rich Glover, Nebraska's nose guard… the ball would be snapped and I could just feel that guy. I actually loved going up to Nebraska, I just wish we were a better team and that we could have been more competitive with them. It's fun to go places where the crowds are intense.

Looking back on it now, during my sophomore year (1971) when the ball would be snapped, everything would happen really fast and I wasn't seeing anything. But by the time I got to my senior year, when the ball was snapped the action was very slow, and I was seeing everything. That's the only way I can describe how things changed. Also, as a sophomore I was around a bunch of older guys—a lot of seniors—and the other quarterback on the team was a senior. A lot of those guys wanted him to be playing. It was pretty uncomfortable.

Don Fambrough on the Band

We had to play to play at Iowa State in 1979—it was the second time I was head coach—and hell, nobody wants to go to Ames, Iowa, and we weren't too good that year. I think we were about a two-touchdown underdog, and the kids were kind of down in the dumps. I went to talk to the band director, Bob Foster. I said, "Bob, this game doesn't mean too much and nobody's going. The band's not going. Is there any way we could probably take a few of the band members up there so we'll have a little backing?" He said, "Well, I've used all my money, I don't know how we'd get there." And I said, "Well, if you think you can round up a few of the band members who want to go, I'll go out and see what we can do to raise some money to get you up there." So he rented an old bus. I think it had "Tonganoxie High School" on it.

I told the players, "Hey, the band's going to be there. We're not going to be alone." And people have always said, "Oh, the band's not that important"—but it is so important to a football team. To any kind of a team, a band is important. Anyway, Foster got a busload of band members to make the trip to Ames. And their bus broke down about a mile outside of the stadium.

My kids are in the dressing room before the game, we've already had the pregame warm up and they think I've lied to them because the band wasn't there—they've got their heads down and we're in terrible shape. Hell, I don't even know if we're going to make it to the kickoff or not. I called one of the assistant coaches and asked, "Where's the band?" And he said, "Coach, there's no band out there."

And all of a sudden, about two or three minutes before it's time for us to go out for the kickoff, we could hear the band. Those band kids had gotten out of that bus, gotten their instruments and marched all the way right up to the door of our dressing room. Well, those players went crazy. Hell, I couldn't control them—they were trying to knock the damn door down. And we went out and won the football game.

After the game, the players came over and they gave me the game ball. John Hadl was on my staff then, and I said, "John, you know what I'm going to do with this ball, don't you?" And he said, "Well, I think I do."

They had our band as far away from the field as they could. So John and I ran to their section with the game ball. All during the game that band played—they never stopped playing. For 60 minutes those band members played KU songs. So I gave the football to the band. Afterward, we got on the airplane and flew back home, but that poor bunch of band guys, they had to wait until the damn bus was fixed. Took 'em all night before they got home.

The next morning at about 7:30, I heard band music outside of my door at my home here in Lawrence. I asked my wife, "Does that sound like a band?" And she said, "It is, there's a band out there." So I got up and I was there in my pajamas and there was the band playing the KU Fight Song—and then they gave me back the football that I'd given them, and each band member had autographed it. Outside of a couple of Missouri game balls, that's the only one I've kept.

Otto Schnellbacher on Coach George Sauer Leaving

Quigley was the Athletic Director at the time I was at KU. Coach Sauer left after the 1947 season and none of us really knew why. We were upset about it because we all liked him so well, and he'd done such a great job. A few years later, after one of the pro games I played in, I spent an evening with him. I asked him, "Coach, why did you leave KU?" He said, "Quigley cut my budget." I couldn't believe it. I know Quigley was that type of guy because when we went to the Orange Bowl, he put the word out that we were only going to take 33 players because we played about 23. He didn't want to take the entire team. I was one of the players who went in and told

Head coach George Sauer talks to his 1947 Jayhawks team. *University of Kansas Archives*

him we weren't going to go unless we took all 53 players, because that was our traveling squad. We had to brow beat him. He said, "You can't do that." I said, "Well, we've just done it. You can call the Orange Bowl and tell them we're not coming unless you take the whole squad." So, we took the whole squad.

That was the start of an athletic director destroying a football program. They brought in J.V. Sikes after that and he did well, but after a period of time, he went down. You can tell I have a little bitterness in my heart about what happened back in those days. Not about losing or winning, but about destroying a football program to cut the budget. And, he did pay off the stadium. He's known for having paid off the stadium. The sad thing is that the program would have been a winner. George Sauer was a winning coach, and he could recruit.

Otto Schnellbacher. *University of Kansas Archives*

Ray Evans on the 1981 Season

It was an interesting year, 1981, if you look back at the scoring for that year. The most points we scored in a game was 27. So we weren't an offensive juggernaut. Kerwin Bell got hurt about the second or third game coming off his huge freshman year. We had a hard time scoring points. Frank Seurer was really getting good. We had a very conservative offense; it was really more of a ball-control offense. We didn't really turn Frank loose until the next year. The offense didn't make mistakes, they didn't turn the ball over. What I think was particularly memorable is that Bucky Scribner was awesome. It was always a battlefield position, which we always won. Our special teams were excellent and Scribner averaged about 44 yards a kick. Kyle McNorton and Chris Toburen really anchored the defensive team. They were seniors and inside backers.

Look at every game (at the scores), and the only game that we didn't play well defensively was at Oklahoma. Other than that, the defense played very, very well. We went to the first game of the year, Tulsa, and Roger Foote picked off a pass, ran 50 yards for a touchdown to win that game. He literally did the same thing the last game of the year against Missouri. It was pretty cool. I think that's really the most consistent Kansas defense I've ever seen for an entire season.

That Missouri game was a blast. I think that was the hardest-hitting Jayhawk defense for one day. Jeremy Coleman hit on a guy, right on our sideline. He just crumbled the guy; the ball popped up and the guy just didn't get up. Plus, we had a lot of Kansas guys on those teams.

Mike Norseth on Playing Nebraska

I think Nebraska was tough. When you walk on the field, you really respect what they have going there. I remember right near the field they had a place for the handicapped people to sit. I thought it was nice that they had a place for the handicapped people to sit and be close to the action. Then I heard someone yell, "Hey, number 7, we're going knock your teeth out!" At that point you know you have to be ready to play.

Another story from the Nebraska game happened in the huddle. In the second quarter—I had been getting pounded pretty good by that time—one of the linemen comes back to the huddle and says to me, "Man, they've got their backup in now, and he's better than the first guy." I said, "Well, that doesn't bode well for me, does it, boys?" That was a long afternoon.

L.T. Levine on the 1995 Season

I think it is a little cocky to say that we believed that was going to happen in 1995. I think we knew the possibilities. We knew who we had on our team, as far as what we had. But we still had a lot of new people. We were switching out quarterbacks, and we had always been a quarterback-driven team. Mark Williams, my roommate the year before, really took over that leadership role. Those two years in between Chip and Mark, we really fell off at that leadership point, and that really hurt us in terms of direction. Chip was more than a football player. He was one of the greatest leaders I've ever played with. He would make guys believe in things that they probably could never

ever do. Mark had that quality, plus he was a great football player also. That '95 season...I still have magazines from that season and I laugh at them. In some of those magazines we were number 76 and 64, and we ended the season number 9 in the country. Just to know how people perceived us before the season and then where we ended up—our final record was 10-2—it was great.

The season was set up for us to be successful. It really came down to all of us learning and meshing with each other and believing in each other, knowing what our capabilities were and what we had as a team. And that really came to fruition, especially in that Oklahoma game. That was the greatest game I had ever been a part of at KU. I didn't even have very great stats. It was the most complete game I ever had. It was one of the biggest atmospheres we had ever played in. It was electrifying that whole night—we beat OU 38-17. It definitely was a testament to how our team was playing at the time, and how we were going to be playing at the end of the year. That was a great year.

Max Ediger on Breaking Curfew

We had a little ceremony when we all moved into the Jayhawk Towers, which was where all the players lived. I'm not sure exactly who initiated what, but we decided we wanted to join our apartments together and shuffle people in and out of the rooms during curfew hours because the coaching staff was pretty strict back then. So Mike Beal brought a Skill saw, and we all passed out hardhats and put them on. We had picture-taking ceremonies when we sawed out the wall in the closet that joined our apartments. We could then crawl from one apartment to the other and easily out of the Towers with-

L.T. Levine. *KUAC Media Relations*

out getting caught. I remember during the cutting "cere-mony," when we were going through the sheet rock, we hit one of those metal beams and sparks were flying all over the place. It was comical because the coaches never figured it out. There were many instances when they said "Go to your own rooms" because it was curfew time, and we'd walk through the closet door and crawl into the other room. They never did figure out what we were doing.

Kelly Donohoe on Playing Auburn

It was just horrible. The thing I remember about that is we knew we were horribly outgunned. Auburn, at that time, was one of the top five or 10 teams of the nation. Not that they aren't now. Back then they were a powerhouse. I remember coming in from pregame and we were dead. The humidity was not something we were used to. We came back from pregame in the locker room and everybody is just sitting around slumped over. I remember thinking, "Oh man. We're in trouble." The game hadn't even started and half our guys were already spent. Needless to say, we just got hammered. One thing I remember—it's kind of fun looking back on now—was something that happened in the third quarter. Gary Huff was our quarterback coach. He was just hired my sopho-more year and led the offense. He was one of those All-America guys at Florida State, and I think he played for the Raiders in the NFL. He took his headphones off when I came to the sidelines and said, "Hey, Kelly. We just need to get a first down." We hadn't gotten a first down since we got the ball. I think the next series we got a couple of first downs. It was just a horrible experience. The thing about it was that going into our junior year, we went back to

Kelly Donohoe. *KUAC Media Relations*

back down at Auburn. I remember Bob Frederick coming up to us in the spring of 1987 (or was it the spring of 1988?) and saying, "Guys, I know that we just played Auburn this year down there, but for financial reasons, we have a chance to go back and play down there again." And, we're going, "Oh, no." We had no say in it. It was already a done deal. I think we made several hundred thousand dollars to travel back down to Auburn, which our program needed. But that was the last place we wanted to go back to. Never again. Before the game our bus drivers are pulling down the tarmac, I think we had just landed. We got on the bus to travel to the airport down to Auburn, and, to this day, we still don't know what happened to the bus driver. But all of a sudden, this bus driver is driving along on the runway area, and there's a plane right there. And the wing is coming at us. He's driving toward the plane that was parked there. And we're like, "Sir? Sir?" He drives right into the wing. And, if it wasn't for him ducking, he would have been decapitated. One of the coaches got up and hit the brake. It was crazy. I don't know if the guy had a seizure or was tired, but he's lucky he didn't get killed.

Chip Budde on the 1986 Oklahoma Game

Before we played Oklahoma in 1986—that was the "Bosworth game"—Chancellor Budig came in and spoke to us before the game. Chancellor Budig is a great guy, he has done fantastic things, but he isn't a great motivational speaker—he's pretty dry. Not the type of guy you want to have talk to the team before a big game. That was pretty funny, and one of my more surreal experiences at KU. We had an administrator, a technocrat, a bureaucrat who is great at what he does, but not the guy you want to have motivating the team in the locker room, and I think he would probably agree with it.

"The University is behind you," he said, "the faculty is behind you, the entire university community is behind you." Try to imagine that without any energy.

Kerwin Bell on Coach Hadl

Coach Fambrough was a great guy, and we got along—I'm just going to say this because it's true. There was sort of an agreement there that Coach Hadl was going to take over the program after our sophomore year. After the success of the Bowl game, I think there was a change of heart. Then after that season, Coach Hadl and three or four other assistants left. Our junior year, 1982, we just fell apart. We had virtually the same people back as far as the talent on offense, and the good, young talent we had on defense was back also. We went from going to a Bowl game into the tank. I think that had to do with players' attitudes about what was supposed to happen and didn't materialize. I think it just carried over mentally.

Mike Hubach on Bicycles

We were playing Oklahoma State at home, it must have been my sophomore year (1977). Somehow during the game, I think I was running down the field on a kick-off coverage, I don't know if I got bumped into and somehow clipped my heal—I actually kicked myself in the left heel—and the thing was really sore. My family was in town from Ohio for the game, and even though we lost, I had a good game, punted pretty

Mike Hubach. *University of Kansas Archives*

well. The next day I could barely walk. Remember, my family was in town, and I was thinking, "What should I do?" I was walking around with my family and thinking that my heel would be okay, so I didn't get any treatment or see the trainer or anything.

Come Monday, I could barely stand on my left foot. This was when Bud Moore was the head coach. We used to start practice off with these quickness drills where you slapped your pads, then slapped your helmets. You'd get in a circle around the coach. Then we'd go kick a couple of field goals, break up and separate into offense and defense groups. And I'd do whatever, go back to kicking, I guess. We did the quickness thing—you know, we'd all grunt "huh, huh, huh," smack our helmets, then smack our pads. When it was time to kick the first field goal, I set up, planted my foot, and almost fell over and kicked the ball on a 30-yard shank job. Coach Moore looked at me—and he had this look—and said, "Son, what's wrong with you?" I'm thinking, "Oh shit," I'm going to get in trouble for not coming into training and putting ice on my heel or whatever. What the heck am I going to say here? I remembered reading in the school newspaper, the *University Daily Kansan*, how people were complaining about bicyclists driving recklessly on campus. So I told Coach Moore I got hit by a bicyclist on campus. He just looked at me.

The headline in the paper the next day was this: Freak happening followed Hubach—Campus Cyclist puts Rush on KU Kicker. And, actually, it was just that I was scared that I didn't come in for treatment. I remembered seeing that in the school paper. I saw Fred Osborne at a get-together the department had for Don Fambrough, and he thought I fell off a barstool. Anyway, I made up a little fib, and I guess that's when I realized I was really somebody on the football team when all these headlines hit the paper.

Nolan Cromwell on Injuring His Knee in the 1976 Oklahoma Game

I cut upfield and got hit by the safety for Oklahoma. It was a freak deal because I went back to the huddle and called the next play. Then I felt my knee start to tighten up and I thought, "Oh man." It didn't really hurt, but it was tightening up. It was difficult to move, so I just held up my hand and jogged off the field. I told the team trainer about it, and the doctor came over, checked it and said it wasn't supposed to wiggle like that. The interesting part is that the injury I had, a little tear in the cartilage and a partial tear in the ligament, in most instances today they would never operate on that. Today it would have healed by itself in about three weeks and I could have been playing again before the season ended. Instead, they opened me up and I have a seven-inch scar from where they repaired it. I was in a cast for seven and a half weeks. Today they would've probably put a little half brace on it and I would've continued to work it and within three weeks I could've been back.

At that point in the game the score was tied: at 10-10, and it was a good game. I think the Oklahoma players probably had some revenge in their minds and hearts and they wanted to get after us. Were they glad I got hurt? Maybe at the point when I got hurt, but after the game they probably wished I hadn't. That's part of the competition. They knew I was a big part of our offense, and if they could get me out of the game, we probably wouldn't be as effective.

CHAPTER 8

Don Fambrough— Bleeding Blue

"I love Don Fambrough. He was the primary reason I went to Kansas."
    —Nolan Cromwell

He is the grand old man of Kansas football, the guy who links the Jayhawks' past with their future. For most of his adult life, Don Fambrough has been a part KU's football program—as a player, assistant coach, head coach and various other roles. So deep is his love and loyalty for Kansas football, you would swear the man must have blue blood—Jayhawk blue.

As a standout player on the Jayhawks' back-to-back Big Six conference co-champions, Fambrough was an excellent, two-time All-Conference guard.

"Don was a tenacious, ferocious, active player," Otto Schnellbacher said of his teammate. "He was all heart."

After serving as an assistant coach for more than two decades at KU—also a few seasons at Wichita State—Fambrough was named as Pepper Rodgers's successor in 1970. He took the Jayhawks to the Liberty Bowl in 1973, but was fired following the 1974 season. Fambrough returned as the head man in 1979, again took KU to a bowl game, only to be let go a year later. Those two downside experiences to his affiliation with the program have not affected his love for KU football. Overall, his record as Kansas's head coach was 36-49-5.

"I've been around too many great kids," Fambrough said of losing his coaching position twice, "been around too many great alums at KU to let something that was a little bit unpleasant overshadow all the good things that happened." He remains an active observer and participant in KU's football fortunes, a regular visitor to all practices who speaks to the team each year before the Missouri game.

Don Fambrough on
Coming to KU as a Student

I started out at Texas University and played my freshman and sophomore years there. Then I went in the service for four years, and I was with Ray Evans, who had been at the University of Kansas before the war, and we became very good friends. We talked about how when we got out we'd probably like to go to school together and

Don Fambrough was an All-Big Six lineman for the 1946-47 Jayhawks. *University of Kansas Archives*

play college football together—and that's the way it turned out. That's how I ended up at KU. It was because of Ray Evans, but he didn't have to twist my arm at all. I fell in love with KU when I came up here for a visit. It was what I'd been looking for. I was born and raised on a ranch down in Texas, and the University of Texas was too big for me. I was just kind of lost down there. The football part I loved, but as far as the school went, it was just way too big. I was excited about the opportunity to come to Kansas and play football with Ray for the remainder of my college career.

Nolan Cromwell on Don Fambrough

I love Don Fambrough. He was the primary reason I went to Kansas. I liked his honesty, he was kind of a good old boy—my type of man. He came out to visit my mom and dad on a recruiting trip. He was very polite, sat down and talked with my parents and me. He made me feel at ease. There wasn't a lot of busy work, he would just sit on the couch and have a piece of pie, talking to us.

It hurt when he was fired after my sophomore season. Going back to when he was recruiting me, he told me that whatever I decided, he had a scholarship for me. If I decided on the signing day or if I wanted to wait until June, he said he would keep a scholarship for me. When they fired him, it was hard to give up the guy who recruited you and everybody else who was there.

Don Fambrough on
Becoming KU's Head Coach

Well you know I was older when I became a head coach, so I guess the biggest thrill I had goes back to when Coach Sikes appointed me head freshman coach. That was the biggest thrill I had, but becoming the head at KU was a great thrill, a great responsibility. It's hard to describe just what the feeling was. You know it's something like being head coach at some other school, but I think that of all the people I've ever known, all the coaches had one goal in mind, and that was someday being head coach of their alma mater where they'd played ball. And to have a chance to be head coach at my school where I'd played, it was a thrill that's hard to explain.

Emmett Edwards on Don Fambrough

First of all, Coach Fambrough ran a good program. He had the ability to break it down to an individual basis if need be. For that alone, everybody admired him—there was hardly a bad word said about him. All the players loved him because you could go talk to him. He was always there to listen to you and to deal with you on an individual basis. He also had a sense of the Jayhawk tradition. He truly admired Kansas and the athletic department.

Chip Budde on
Fambrough's Motivational Speeches

Running up the score or getting the score run up on you—that's the nature of the rivalry, or as Coach Fambrough would say "The nature of the war." That was the speech he gave to us in 1988. He said, "You have your damn rivalry. Your rivalry is with Kansas State. This is a war! Playing Missouri is a war that goes back to the 1860s." Then he spun in some flavor with a few more things about the history and meaning of the game, stuff to try to motivate the guys on the team. I really liked it when he said, "You want to be on the side of righteousness and purity." That was the Kansas side, of course.

Don Fambrough on Recruiting

I love recruiting and that's something that a lot of coaches hate. In fact, a lot of coaches get out of the business because they hate to recruit. I always really enjoyed recruiting. I loved it. To me, when you sign a good kid, you know a John Riggins or someone like that, who says he wants to come to the University of Kansas, it's almost like winning a football game. I've always been involved with recruiting—when I was head coach, when I was assistant coach. I remember when Coach Sikes hired me the first time back in 1949, he said, "There are two things I want you to do, Don. Number one, I've made arrangements for you to go down and spend two weeks in Alabama during their spring practice to see what they're doing. And then when you get back, I want you to spend a lot of time with Phog Allen and talk about recruiting."

I'll never forget what Dr. Allen told me. "Now Don, when you go out to recruit, you want to recruit the mothers," he said. "Be nice to the father, but you really want to spend a lot of time with the mother, because she's the one who's going to make the final decision. For 18 years she's told that kid what to do, and she'll end up telling him where to go to school." I never forgot that. Phog was one of the very best at recruiting that there ever was.

Max Ediger on Harassing Assistant Coaches

We once locked Clayton Williams, one of the assistant coaches, in his room. Clayton was the freshman coach and was required to live in the same quarters as the student athletes. He was supposed to watch over us, protect us, make sure we were all tucked in at night. We had problems with him throughout the year because we lived above him and he would always complain that we were too loud. In the middle of the season, one of the players bought a chain-link fence with a couple of padlocks on it. We found out about it and got the keys from him and, unbeknownst to him, took it off. When we heard that Coach Moore was terminated, that night the padlocks and chain went back on the door, Clayton's door. We got up the next morning and there was this ruckus about how we were off the team, we were out of the Towers. We realized it was only Clayton, so we all went back to bed. We went down to lunch—we'd had a long night of partying—and there was a sign that said: "Calovich, Beal, Murphy, Wellman, Ediger. Please report to Coach Fambrough's office." Fam was the head coach again.

We all went down there together after lunch. We congratulated Coach Fambrough on getting his old job back. He was the head coach when we were freshmen, recruited all of us, brought us to KU. After a lot of "How are yous?" and "I'm fines," Fam said, "By the way, which one of you guys locked Clayton in his room?" We were all kind of pointing at each other. Nobody would take responsibility for it. So he just said, "Don't be locking Clayton in his room." I about busted a gut when we found out what happened, which was this: Clayton had to call the fire department to come get him out of his room and he was late for his coaches' meeting. Of course, Fambrough was probably all over him, wondering why he was late. That's one thing you don't do, be late to a meeting.

Curtis McClinton on Don Fambrough

Coach Fambrough was my line coach at Wichita and he kept me on the line. I was an offensive/defensive end. I liked the position, and I knew the position. I fared reasonably well in competition both offensively and defensively as a freshman. When I matriculated back to KU, Coach Fambrough was there with head coach Jack Mitchell, and I'm not altogether sure that Coach Fambrough ever gave up on me being a lineman, specifically on defense, because he had me all over the line, even over the center. Coach Mitchell was very knowledgeable about players and their abilities, and he was aware of my hurdling and good speed, so eventually I ended up in the backfield with John Hadl, who was an All-American at halfback and also an All-American at quarterback. And I was All-America at fullback. Coach Fambrough was not only a good coach, but he was a mentor on the academic side in regard to focusing on scholarship and graduating from KU.

I had the privilege of going to the Tangerine Bowl with him and what a great experience it was to travel with the ball club. I was invited by Lou Perkins, who is an excellent athletic director and is really very focused. It was good being with Coach Fambrough and watching the practices, being able to talk to him about his outstanding achievements at KU and when he took the team to the Liberty Bowl.

Kelly Donohoe on Fambrough's Pregame Speeches

I will never forget my junior year, the 1988 season. Coach Mason had Don Fambrough come talk to us before the Missouri game, and he gave a stirring speech. It was about Jayhawkers and Quantrell and all that happened between the states of Missouri and Kansas. We were ready to go up and bust down a wall—then we went out and got beat 55-17. I will never forget that. We were one and nine going into that game, but we really felt that we were going to end our season on a great note and beat Missouri. Then they drubbed us. Fambrough really lit us up, though, and then we just played horrible.

Ray Evans on Fambrough and His Coaches

I don't know what I expected when Coach Fambrough took over the team again. I think everybody was so excited to have somebody who was so positive and upbeat. Anybody would have looked upbeat and positive after what we went through, because there was so much brow-beating going on beforehand, but it was even better with Coach Fambrough. He was one of the best salesmen you'll ever see in your life. I really, honestly believe this, there was not a game, and I'm totally serious when I say this, there was not a game when Coach Fambrough was there that he didn't have at least me believing that we were going to win. And that it is really unusual when you think of some of the outmanned games we played in. He could just talk you into it—"Here's the scenario and how we're going to win." He was great at it. You could tell he was really good right away because he surrounded himself with an excellent coaching staff. Kent Stephenson had been really successful at Oklahoma State. Mike Sweatman was already a great KU name, and it was fun to have him back. I was pretty excited. It was a very good staff. And it was just so different than what we had been used to and it was so fun to have something that upbeat and positive. You could see yourself getting better. You could feel yourself getting better. It was exciting, and people were becoming galvanized.

Mike Hubach on the 1979 Media Guide

I didn't know how big a part of the team I really was until they put me on the cover of the Jayhawk media guide. They had John Hadl, Riggins, Douglas, Sayers, Zook, Jaynes, Cromwell—and they had a picture of me on this thing. That shocked me. That was really something to be on the press guide and poster for the year. Coach Fambrough thought so much about me that he put me on that guide. It was kind of like a smack in my face, like, whoa. It was something.

Don Fambrough on
His Most Exciting Moments

I guess going to the Liberty Bowl in 1973 was one of my biggest thrills as a head coach. We'd been told that we would be considered, but we had to beat Missouri. And I never will forget during the game, Missouri was six points ahead of us in the fourth quarter. We were in a situation where we had fourth and long—I forget the exact yardage—and we called timeout. David Jaynes came over on the sideline and Charlie McCuller was my offensive coordinator, and we talked about it. We had to make a decision to either punt the ball and hope we could get it back, or go for the first down and keep the football. I think Charlie wanted to kick the ball. Finally I asked David— just the two of us—and I said, "David, what do you want to do? Tell me what you'd like to do." He said, "Coach, let me throw the football." I said all right, throw the ball.

We went for the first down. Missouri was pretty sure we'd throw to Emmett Edwards—our best receiver—and they had double coverage on him. Emmett goes down the sideline, and I can still see the play now because it was impossible for him to catch the ball. He was completely surrounded by the Missouri players. But David threw the ball and Emmett went up high off—it was thrown high— and came down with the football. We got the first down and we went on and scored and won the football game. And we're in the dressing room and they come tell me that I have a phone call, and that it's a pretty important call so I better take it. And it's the Liberty Bowl committee extending the invitation to KU to play in their game. That probably was the most exciting football game as a head coach I was involved in.

The Jayhawks give Coach Fambrough a ride off the field after defeating Missouri in 1973. *University of Kansas Archives*

Max Ediger on Playing for Fambrough

The way I saw it was that everybody loved Fambrough. He had a 4-7 season, and they ended up firing the guy, even though he was coming off the Liberty Bowl the previous year. As a freshman, you don't really think about it, and being a non-scholarship player, I didn't have a voice in the decision, obviously. It was kind of a shock, I think, that he got fired. Most people will tell you that Coach Fambrough was the greatest coach you could possibly have because he cared about his players. He knew your names, he knew how to pronounce them—little things like that.

Then they brought in Bud Moore from Alabama. He definitely had a lot of fire in him, but the one thing I can say after I played four seasons under him is that I respect-

ed the guy because I loved playing the game and I think he was a good fundamentals coach. I think the area that he was really lacking was in the basic skills of communication, and not only with his players, but also his coaches. I think the worst thing that happened was having that really good season his first year, and beating Oklahoma. I think his ego got away from him. I felt a distance between him, the coaching staff and the players. He obviously took the same players that Fambrough recruited and turned them into a winning team under the Bear Bryant offensive scheme. His recruiting skills weren't nearly as good as Fambrough's and it showed over the years, which led to his demise. Not only recruiting, but I felt the distance that he had between himself and his players and coaches took its toll in the end. I don't think the players played for him as well as they just wanted to win, just because they were at KU. It wasn't like that for Fambrough—you wanted to play for the guy because you liked him.

CHAPTER 9

Postseason Glory— Bowl Games

"I feel the Orange Bowl was a tremendous thing for our football team, for our fans, for our students, for everybody involved, and everybody is involved here."
—Pepper Rodgers, *1969 Jayhawker Yearbook*

The success of most college football teams is easily measured: How many bowl games has the school played in? For KU that number currently stands at nine, and while that's a small number compared to some schools, Jayhawk fans—knowing the number should be larger—can still be proud of the teams from many different eras that have played in postseason games.

Kansas appeared in its first bowl following the 1947 season, losing a heartbreaker to Georgia Tech in the Orange Bowl. KU landed in the Bluebonnet Bowl following the 1961 season, and beat up a good Rice squad, 33-7. The Jayhawks lost a sobering heartbreaker to Penn State in the 1969 Orange Bowl—the infamous 12th man game.

After losing bowl games in 1973, 1975 and 1981, Kansas finally hit postseason pay dirt with a win in the 1992 Aloha Bowl. They repeated the feat in 1995, and capped a great turnaround season in 2003 with an appearance in the Tangerine Bowl.

Otto Schnellbacher on the 1948 Orange Bowl

The 1948 Orange Bowl was kind of exciting because it was the first time that KU had ever gone to a Bowl. We had tied Oklahoma for the championship in the Big Six. In the game, Georgia Tech got us down a little bit—we were behind two touchdowns—then we finally got a score in. With about five minutes to go, they still had the ball, but we held them and got the ball back. We were down 20-14, but we began to march down the field, and I caught a pass on about the 40-yard line. They called me out of bounds on the 10. I may have been out of bounds, but I didn't think I was. Hell, I used the official as a blocker and shoved him into some people. The next play, Ray Evans went nine yards. Now, it's second and goal at the one. The snap from center wasn't very good, and Lynn McNutt, our quarterback, went down on the ball and we were yelling at the official to blow the whistle—he never blew it—and they took the ball away from him when he was on the ground. Georgia Tech came up with the ball, and that cost us the game. In my mind, I feel that we got two bad calls in the last minutes of the ball-game. My catch and run that was called out of bounds, and then when they wouldn't blow the whistle when McNutt went down on the ball. At the 50-year reunion of the Orange Bowl that I went to in Miami, the Georgia Tech people were there and they admitted they had pulled his arms apart and taken the ball away when he was down. So, we should have won that one, but we didn't—it would have been a great event. But it was good for Kansas because the program was built.

Don Fambrough (number 22 in white) and Otto Schnellbacher (behind him) look on during the pregame activities at the 1948 Orange Bowl against Georgia Tech. *University of Kansas Archives*

Don Fambrough on
the 1948 Orange Bowl

Otto Schnellbacher and I were co-captains of the football team and our last game was with the University of Arizona in Tucson. We were having our pregame meal at 9:00 on Saturday morning before our 1:00 game. Somebody came into the dining room and they delivered a telegram to Otto and me—it was from E. C. Quigley, who was the athletic director at KU. And this telegram said, "Congratulations, the University of Kansas has been selected to play in the Orange Bowl." Well, we read that and oh, we got so excited. I remember George Sauer was madder than hell. You know, golly, we're going to lose this game. You know the kids would be thinking about the Orange Bowl. We're going to get beat by Arizona and that'd be a disgrace. So we were really excited about the opportunity to go to the Orange Bowl, but we did beat Arizona, which gave us an undefeated season—we did have two ties. That was the first time that KU had ever played in a bowl game. There was so much excitement on the campus and everybody was making plans to go to Miami. So that was a great thing, great memories of that occasion.

I think we got down there about a week before the game. There was a rule that you were expected to be there so many days before the game so you could have a lot of press conferences and that sort of thing. We were a more mature group of people, excited about playing but not overly excited. And it was a hell of a football game. Of course we should have won. I think that in the game we were six points behind and we took the ball on our own 10- or 15-yard line and we ran the Evans right, the Evans left and the Evans up the middle and then an Evans pass to Schnellbacher. We moved it down to their one-yard line and had first and goal with 58 seconds left to play. That's when we fumbled the ball on the one-yard line.

Was it a fumble by McNutt? Yeah, he fumbled the ball. I don't know who came up with it. I can remember to this day that there was a pile of bodies there—about six or seven feet deep—and nobody would move. The official couldn't get anybody to move. Finally, he just turned and said it was Georgia Tech's ball. I think he just had to make a decision and that's the decision he made. We don't think to this day that it was their ball, but maybe that's wishful thinking.

Bert Coan on
the 1961 Bluebonnet Bowl

Oh, the team wasn't going to play in that Bluebonnet Bowl. I wasn't playing because I'd broken my leg. Still, I got up and made a speech to the team—I'm from the Houston area—and I said that it was a first-class bowl game and that they needed to play in it. The team was going to vote against playing, everyone was talking against it, saying it was a second-class game, which it wasn't. That was one of the few speeches I ever made in my life, getting them to go to Houston for that game. And they were all glad they did when it was over, since it turned out to be a real good deal. They ended up beating Rice 33 to 7.

Of course, I did go to Houston to cheer on the guys. I was sitting behind the KU bench at the Bluebonnet Bowl game with Bud Adams (owner of the Tennessee Titans who flew me to Chicago) and he had this old box camera. I said to myself, "Now there's a very rich man and he's got this old granny-looking box camera." Well, a few minutes later he unscrewed the top of the camera and took a drink from it. It was full of scotch! It wasn't a camera at all, it just looked like one.

John Hadl on
the 1961 Bluebonnet Bowl

Yeah, Bert (Coan) gave a speech to the team concerning the Bluebonnet Bowl. He wanted to go back to Houston, that's all that was. Everyone voted on it. I actually wanted to go and play, but there were a lot of guys who didn't want to because of work, Christmas break, etc. We were really glad, obviously, that we decided to play the game. And Bert was right, it was a good time, and it was a big-time deal for us.

Jack Mitchell on
the 1961 Bluebonnet Bowl

This was the key play of the game: We were in punt formation and Johnny Hadl went back to punt the ball. The game was real close, we were having a little trouble rushing the passer. We changed at the half and picked it up a little. And that's where we beat them, in the second half. But the key play of the game was when Hadl went back to punt and the snap was low. I think he had to reach down to get it and it either hit the ground or slipped out of his hands. He picked it up and started to kick it, but he couldn't kick it because they were right there on top of him. So he just spun around and had a wide-open field, ran outside and right down the field. John had a lot of talent—he could run, kick and pass. He was a great leader and a wonderful guy.

Jack Mitchell gets a ride following KU's 33-7 win over Rice in the Bluebonnet Bowl. *University of Kansas Archives*

Bobby Douglas on the 1969 Orange Bowl

I remember just being excited that we made it to the Orange Bowl. Obviously, we wanted to win the game. You are always trying to win. As I remember it today, I didn't make it the most important thing in my life. I knew I was going to play professional football. I was invited to all the All-Star games that year so I was looking at the Orange Bowl as "Let's win the game, play well and all that." So, when the game was over, I was going to play another game three days later. As upset as I was at losing the Orange Bowl, life goes on, especially in my situation. I think it probably hit a lot of other guys worse than it did me. I'm very competitive, but when a game is over, you've got to move on. We didn't play a good offensive game. The reason was because they had two All-America tackles who killed us. They were very quick. Penn State had about 10 guys who played professional football off that team.

The only thing I really remember is that we should probably have kicked a field goal late in the game. We played it a little conservative because we pretty much moved the ball down and got into position to kick the field goal. We were ahead. We went for it and didn't get it. They came back and scored.

As for the 12th man penalty play, I did watch that because that was on TV forever. The fact is those are mistakes that happen in football. To me it wasn't anything other than "too bad." The bottom line is, I think we could have won the game.

Pepper Rodgers on the 1969 Orange Bowl

The game was a thrill for the players and me. The thing about the game that made it so unusual was the 12 guys on the field at the end of the game. What's interesting about that is we were leading the game 14-7 and Penn State didn't have any timeouts left. They had the ball at their 40-yard line. Dave McClain, one of my assistant coaches, sent an extra linebacker in for defensive tackle so we'd be defending the pass with one more person. On the third down of that series, they threw a long pass and this guy jumped up in the air at about the 5-yard line and caught the ball. McClain grabbed Carl Salb and sent him back into the game. Salb's about 270 and it's a pretty good run from the sidelines to the five-yard line. Salb ran into the game and didn't tell Rick Abernathy to come up, he

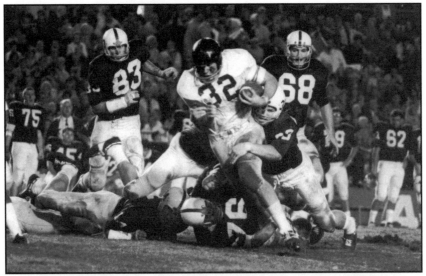

John Riggins (number 32) struggles for yardage against Penn State in the 1969 Orange Bowl. *University of Kansas Archives*

just lined up. They ran plays, scored on fourth down. They went for two and didn't make it. The game was over—it was then they noticed the twelfth guy. He'd been on the field for five plays. The officials didn't catch it. If they'd been doing their job, if they would've called the penalty when it originally happened, we would've won the game.

Nolan Cromwell on the 1973 Liberty Bowl

It was interesting from the standpoint that the season was extremely long for me. Coming from high school, the season usually ends by the first weekend of November. You're playing a full season of football, plus going to a bowl game, which was in the middle of December. It was a long year, but it was fun. We wish we

KU fullback Robert Miller (number 32) leads the way for Delvin Williams in the 1973 Liberty Bowl. *University of Kansas Archives*

would've won the Liberty Bowl of course, but it was a good game.

Emmett Edwards on the 1973 Liberty Bowl

We were down there earlier in the season (Tennessee, in Knoxville) playing the University of Tennessee, and we wanted to go back. We went down to Memphis and had a good time. The weather didn't turn out very good, it ended up being really chilly the night of the game. North Carolina State was a good team, their coach (Lou Holtz), was an outstanding coach and he had his players well prepared. We were unable to beat them, but it was a really good game. It was a good bowl game to go to.

David Jaynes on the 1973 Liberty Bowl

It was fun playing in the Bowl, but the thing that bothers me even to this day is that we weren't really prepared for the game. We should've been, but we weren't, and we could have beaten those guys. It had nothing to do with the cold or anything like that. It was a lot of fun going down there. Another thing was the "special jerseys" we had to wear for the game. All season long we wore white jerseys and blue pants in our away games. In the bowl game, they designed this ugly jersey with kind of a blue yoke on the shoulders and "KANSAS" on the front. And we wore white pants instead of blue. I thought that jersey was horrible. I don't know who made that decision. I felt like, "What? You want us to wear this stuff?" We should have just come out wearing the same uniform we'd been wearing all year.

Nolan Cromwell on the 1975 Sun Bowl

Going to the Sun Bowl, we were really excited to be playing in the game. We were playing Pittsburgh, and I really felt that we could win. Early in the game, we ran our option play to the left. I ended up pitching it out to Billy Campfield just before I got tackled, and he went about 70 yards for a touchdown. But it was called back because they ruled it a forward pitch. That kind of took a little bit out of us and we never really got back in sync or back on track. Pittsburgh had a very good team, and they ended up winning the National Championship the following season.

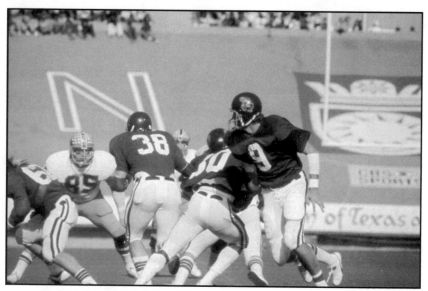

Nolan Cromwell hands off to Laverne Smith in the 1975 Sun Bowl. *University of Kansas Archives*

Kerwin Bell on
the 1981 Hall of Fame Bowl

That was disappointing, not getting to play with the team in the game in Birmingham. I went back home and watched it with my parents. I guess when you're that young, you're thinking: why me? You know, of course, that it's just part of the game. I was never hurt before, playing five years of junior All-America football and four years of high school. It was disappointing because I started so strong and then I had to come back off of it. And it would have been nice if the team would have won the game.

Don Davis on the 1992 Aloha Bowl

I had never been outside the states before. I guess Hawaii is a state, but it felt like going to a whole new country for me. It was great weather compared to Kansas in December. We all rented scooters and drove them all over the islands. It was just a lot of fun. It was interesting seeing the BYU guys, because they were all older. Most of them had wives or kids, and they were all grown men because of the Mormon culture. We felt like we were playing a professional team. I know they got up on us, but we came back and won. It was a great feeling to win on national television on Christmas day. I'll always remember that bowl game.

Coach, I Gotta Go!

As the Jayhawks were driving late in the game for what would be the game-winning score in the 1992 Aloha Bowl, KU kicker Dan Eichloff approached Coach Mason.

"Coach, I've got to go to the bathroom."

Mason said no way was he leaving the field. Kansas was in scoring position, and Eichloff might have to go in and kick soon. The kicker held his own, so to speak, and soon trotted onto the field to boot a game-winning field goal from 48 yards.

Final score: Kansas 23, BYU 20.

"Dan asked me if he had time to go to the bathroom," Mason said after the game. "I told him he didn't or he'd have to go in his pants."

Chip Hilleary on the 1992 Aloha Bowl

The Aloha Bowl. My fondest memory of playing at Kansas was being able to go to Hawaii with 75 of my closest friends, and everything we worked toward for four years to finally be accomplished and reap the rewards. Coach Mason had a great perspective on it. He wanted to reward us on top of being able to play in the game. He wanted to allow us to have some flexibility and freedom to enjoy the week in Hawaii and the game. It was very enjoyable from the standpoint that it wasn't just about football. We did some neat things. We got to go to the children's hospital. We got space in the parades. All those things that were fun to do, yet he also allowed some flexibility to enjoy ourselves at night. We practiced hard and we played hard. Then, for the game to turn out the way it did—that was what we were about. I think that Kansas football at that time, we thought of ourselves as being tough and being winners. To be able to go out with a win our senior year for all the hard work we'd put in over four years, and to have Dan Eichloff put it through the uprights to win the game at the end was great.

I think with a minute or a minute and a half left in the game, Dan asked Coach Mason if he could go to the bathroom. Coach Mason told him no. Actually, Coach said something a little stronger than that.

Eichloff was a mental kicker. Most people talk about kickers being a different breed, and he was definitely one of those guys who, if he didn't do the exact same thing every time, it would throw him off. I had a routine that I would go through with him mentally, and I would say the same words every time, I would do the same thing and he was Mr. Consistency. If you didn't say the right thing or do the exact same procedure every time it was like night and day, and he wasn't nearly as consistent.

Stubblefield Excels

Dana Stubblefield, KU's talented senior defensive tackle, played the game of his life against BYU in the 1992 Aloha Bowl. He recorded three sacks for a minus 22 yards.

"That was the best," Stubblefield said following the game. "That game right there was the best that I played. It was an afternoon any senior would have loved. To finish like we did was one of the best feelings that any football player can experience."

Stubblefield was named Kansas's outstanding player of the game for his performance.

L.T. Levine on the 1992 Aloha Bowl

It was the first time I had been to Hawaii, and that was cool. Just to see everything like you see it on TV. To feel the weather, it was just like paradise basically. And playing the game coupled with the whole week of preparation for the game, it was exciting. It was also nerve-wracking. I don't think I slept an ounce the night before the game, because I knew I was going to play a lot more than I had all year. I was pretty amped up. My family was going to be there, and I knew my friends back at home would be watching. It was the only game that was going to be on Christmas day. Going into the game, I think I only threw up once or twice.

Dana Stubblefield (left) poses with BYU's Tom Young after the 1992 Aloha Bowl. Stubblefield was named KU's most outstanding player of the game. *KUAC Media Relations*

Jason Thoren on the 1995 Aloha Bowl

We found out at about 6 a.m. the day of the Aloha Bowl game that Coach Mason wasn't going to Georgia. We had a very early team meeting, because the game over there started at like 9 or 10 in the morning. And that was when he came in and told us. He just said, "I've decided to stay. You guys are my team, and we've come a long way together." In the back of his mind it was the right decision to stay, and it was best for us. And that made us extremely happy.

I remember looking at those guys on the beach, the UCLA players, and we had team functions together. The longer we were on that island the more we were starting to dislike them. Two nights before the game there was a dinner that kind of got out of hand. Players started standing up, and there was almost a fight. Coach Mason stood up and calmed everybody down. I remember him saying something about hoping that we hadn't just written checks that were going to bounce. When Christmas day rolled around, we wanted to demolish them. And we did.

L.T. Levine on the 1995 Aloha Bowl

It was just like David and Goliath. They had Jonathon Ogden, and after Gilbert Brown, he was one of the biggest guys I'd ever seen. Karem Abdul-Jabbar was one of the best running backs in the nation. They had Donnie Edwards. They had some pretty good guys. They weren't as good as some of the classic UCLA teams, but they were a still a good team. It was a nice, beautiful day. It was the second time being there for some of us. We were more comfortable with the field and the atmosphere. It was easier for us to adjust to the heat as well. We just had a better game plan than they were expecting. We jumped on them and just stayed on them, just kept pounding them.

Spencer Bonner on
the 1995 Aloha Bowl

Coach Mason announced he was going to stay at Kansas in a team meeting after we had warmed up—he was not going to go to Georgia, had changed his mind and was going to stay at KU. For the first half of that game, he said that since he had previously committed to leaving and going to Georgia, he decided to let the coordinators coach the first half of the game. He wasn't going to have any input in the first half of the game. The second half, Mason resumed control over the offense and all the plays. A lot of guys were happy about him making that decision. The turmoil that was going on at that time, it was over with. This was the coach who would be there next year. They didn't have to worry about a new guy showing up here and maybe changing things around. At that point, a lot of people were happy about that. June Henley really liked Coach Mason and he had mentioned that if Mason left that he would try to go pro or transfer. He was a big Mason guy.

Bill Whittemore on
the 2003 Tangerine Bowl

I was thrilled that we got the bowl game. We had to wait until the last Big 12 game had been played. For two days straight over Thanksgiving, I was glued to SportCenter, hoping to catch some news, and also checking the internet. Coach Mangino and Mr. Perkins (KU's athletic director) were pretty confident we were going to get it, but it's just like anything else. They were in it for their best interests, and they wouldn't be afraid to swipe it away from us and give it to somebody else.

When we did get the bid, it was awesome. I got five phone calls from teammates immediately—"Did you see? Did you see it?" Playing in a bowl game was something I've always wanted to do, and I feel like my college career was a success now. It was a big step for KU to go from 2-10 to six wins and a bowl game. Everybody had a great time in Orlando, and hopefully the players still on the team will have the opportunity to experience something like again.

CHAPTER 10

Glen Mason— His Way

"What Coach Mason did for me in my life was incredible, because he took a guy who was coming off a horrible sophomore season at quarterback and believed in me. I remember what that meant to me, the confidence he gave me in myself— I owe him so much for that."
—Kelly Donohoe

It wasn't exactly a dream job, and most observers probably considered it an unworkable nightmare. When Glen Mason took over as KU's new head coach the last week of December in 1987, the Jayhawks were coming off what was arguably the team's worst season ever. Kansas had won just four games in two years, and if it hadn't been for cross-state rival K-State, would have been considered the worst Division One program in the country.

"An attitude had set in that we couldn't win," Mason said of his first year at KU, "and that we couldn't make it."

It took a while, but everything changed.

Beginning with a grueling off-season program that flushed out the soft and apathetic players who didn't want to be there, Mason then infused a sense of toughness and fire in his players. By his third season the Jayhawks were competitive, they had a winning record his fourth year, and in 1992 Kansas capped a memorable season by earning a bid to the Aloha Bowl. Three years later the Jayhawks finished 10-2, demolished UCLA in the Aloha Bowl and were the number-nine ranked team in the country at the end of the season.

"I might have pissed some people off along the way, but that probably had to be done," Mason said following the 1995 season. "This program is probably a whole lot better now than it was when I came in 1988."

Mason left KU to take the head coaching position at the University of Minnesota following the 1996 season.

Not a Promising Introduction

When Glen Mason was introduced as the new coach at the University of Kansas, he wasn't exactly ushered in in a grand manner. There were no parades, parties or jubilant fans clamoring about the press conference. In fact, Mason felt the entire press conference was held in an air of unfriendliness. The attitude at KU, at least concerning football, was very bad.

"The things I want to concentrate on are the things we can control immediately," he said at the press conference. "The No. 1 thing we have to change is attitude. We're going to go to work on that. We will change the attitude."

Chip Budde on
Glen Mason Taking Over

Night and day, or day and night, good to evil? I
don't know. It sure was a change when Coach
Mason took over. He shocked the system. There were still
a lot of tourists left who were just cruising through. You
know they weren't there to get an education and play good
football. But we lost a lot of guys during Mason's first six
months. We lost 15 to 20 guys during his first winter. He
came in December and once recruiting was over, we were
doing winter conditioning drills and they were tough. If he
didn't like what we were doing, we got up at 6:00 in the
morning to run the hill. It wasn't very fun. I actually had a
ligament tear on my knee and missed his first spring. So I
actually missed a couple of the 14th Street hill runs. Coach
Mason still made me get up and watch them run, but he
wasn't giving any slack and rightfully so.

We had a lot of guys who needed to test their commitment to the program. I was never a guy who enjoyed running and never did well. His first fall, I was up at 6:00
every morning during two-a-days because I didn't make
my time. I questioned whether or not I wanted to be there.
It wasn't fun. He put so much emphasis on running and
making times, because that's the way to do it. So much
emphasis on that, that we had offensive linemen who were
at 240 pounds because they were more concerned with
making their time than they were with being competitive
on the football team. And that hurt Coach Mason. We
were 1 and 10 that year. We were small. He boiled the pot
down—the smaller the number, the stronger the individual, that was his philosophy. One day we lost half of our
defense. Like four guys quit. We called it Black Monday.
That first year was pretty rough.

Chip Budde, 13. *KUAC Media Relations*

Don Davis, on Mason's Big Games

I think beating Oklahoma in 1992 was one of the biggest games for us, because we hadn't beaten them in a while. We had high expectations, but we had lost a night game to California, so we still had a lot to prove. By the time of the Oklahoma game, we were really clicking as a team. To beat Oklahoma was just huge. The other game that stands out is almost beating Nebraska in 1993. I know that it is kind of strange to have your claim to fame be almost beating someone, but I will never forget that game. I remember they blew a coverage on the two-point conversion at the end or we would have won. It was memorable because we were having a bad year, and nobody expected anything out of us.

Another big game, though, was at Iowa State in 1992. We came from behind to beat them 50-47. That was a game where we really let down and then came back. Of course they had that running back Troy Davis, who played in the NFL, and he scored a lot of points. They jumped out on us, and we were wondering what was going on. That whole season was just great, though. A play here or a play there, and we realistically could have had a one-loss season. The only team that beat us handily was Nebraska. I remember that game well. It was freezing up there, and they just took it to us.

L.T. Levine on
Glen Mason's Coaching Style

Coach Mason was very vicious and savvy with his coaching style—he wanted it done his way. I respected it, and some guys respected it, but some guys didn't. He ran his type of ship, and I learned a lot from him on and off the field. He was a great mentor to me, especially since he and I grew up in the same area, New Jersey. He was really good at helping me adjust to Kansas, knowing where I came from.

Kelly Donohoe on Glen Mason

We were one of the worst divisional programs, but it was still Division One football. We didn't walk around every day with our heads down. When Mason came in, there was a lot of pride in knowing that this program was getting better. We didn't view ourselves as the bottom-of-the barrel program. Mason instilled the belief that we were a competitive football team, and that's the attitude we had. It wasn't like that with Coach Valesente—that was just a really miserable time. There was optimism with Mason. Those 1988-89 seasons really evened out the tough times that 1986-87 brought. 1988-89 was fun, and they were competitive. Things were going in the right direction and it was only going to go better.

Don Davis on Glen Mason

I always thought of Coach Mason as a politician. He should run for office, because he definitely has the charisma of a politician. He was always true to his word, and he really knew how to motivate guys on a different level—he was more than just Xs and Os. He gets you to more of an intellectual level. We always used to joke about how he talked, too. He had this little "hmmm" in his voice, and a lot of the guys used to make fun of that. The other

Things were difficult for Glen Mason his first two seasons at Kansas. *University of Kansas Archives*

thing about Mason was that you either liked him or hated him. There really was no in between. You were either his guy and you were cool, or you would butt heads with him. Fortunately, I was one of the guys that got along with him.

Chip Hilleary on the 1992 Aloha Bowl

There's no doubt that the biggest game that will always stick out in my mind is the Aloha Bowl my senior year. This is one of the most watched college football games for the sheer fact that on Christmas day, there's nothing else to do after opening presents. It was a good way to cap off a career. My senior year of high school, Kansas and Kansas State went from the two worst college football teams in the nation to being ranked in the top 25 the majority of my senior year. It's really a feather in the cap to what Coach Mason was trying to do with the program, that it had finally hit the national limelight.

Kelly Donohoe on Mason's changes

It was very encouraging when Mason came in because he brought with him a team atmosphere. There was a feel of team again, even though when he came in he ran a boot camp program and ran a lot of people off. He was going to get rid of those guys who didn't really have the heart to commit to the program. The attrition rate that first off season was unbelievable. And it was tough because some of my very best friends left. But I did know that he was going to bring a winning attitude because he just had that energy and that spark that you could feel and I knew good things were coming. It was something that we hadn't felt the previous two years. He took a group that had the least talent of any of the teams in the two previous years under Coach Valesente.

Mason's first year, 1988, I think we were 1 and 10, but most of the games were close. Then, in the third or fourth quarter, we would just be outmanned. But at least we knew where we were going. My senior year, 1989, we were 4 and 7. The wheels were turning in the right direction. He recruited some really good players, Stubblefield and Gilbert Brown, so you knew good things were going to happen. I remember thinking in 1989, "I just wish I had another year." I remember petitioning for another year because I lost my redshirt when there were three games left [my freshman year]. It was really a disappointment because I played three games at the end of that season. I think the way the redshirt works is that if you'd played early in a season, you could redshirt. It's hard to get a redshirt back or play an additional season if you played late in the season.

Chip Budde on the Helmet Slap

Kevin Verdugo was was an option quarterback in high school and did not want to be an option quarterback in college. He came into KU ready to be a drop-back passer, and he was a good one. Mason came in and he ran pure college offense. He kept the ball on the ground and expected the quarterback to be able to run. That was not what Kevin signed up for, so he said he was going to leave, but he would finish out the academic year at KU and continue practicing with the team because we were short bodies and we needed him. That is the most selfless thing that I have heard of in college sports. He was doing it for the guys he had played with for a year and a half. He was out there and didn't have to be.

During practice, I think Kevin made the same mistake twice in a passing drill and Coach Mason smacked him upside the head. It wasn't a big deal, you have so much body armor on that it would take a baseball bat to really hurt you. If you are worried about some 45-year-old guy smacking you upside the head, then you are in the wrong business. Coach Mason wasn't a nice guy, he knew what he wanted. Of course coaches yell to get the point across, and he just smacked him upside the head. If he wanted to hurt Kevin, he would have punched him in the stomach where he didn't have any padding. It was not a sign of an abusive relationship, but someone from the press probably saw it. Mason had lost a lot of guys, it was his first season. He came from Ohio State and played for Woody Hayes. I think it was the fact that Mason came from a program that was abusive to its players. If Mason would have come from anywhere else, it wouldn't have been an issue. Kevin walked out of practice because of that. I talked to him that night and it wasn't a big deal, and Kevin came back to practice. Tempers flared, then tempers cooled. But the flame continued to be fanned by the people who watched the program.

L.T. Levine on Mason Taking the Georgia Job

I was a senior, so I wasn't too concerned about Coach Mason going to Georgia, leaving the program. But there were still loyalty issues. We all knew that Coach Mason was business-minded in a sense. It wasn't totally surprising, but it was heartbreaking because we felt that he had done so much to build what he had at KU. Not to see it finished through was disheartening. We felt that he was leaving at the wrong time. We felt that there was more that he could have done at Kansas. That morning when he told us he was staying, it didn't matter who you put in front of us. We were going to win. Everyone was pretty amped up. That whole week was confusing in a sense—we knew he was going, but he was there the whole week. Guys were wondering about transferring and what they were going to do. But once we found out he was staying, then everybody was extremely happy.

Spencer Bonner on Mason Taking the Georgia Job

Coach Mason announced he was leaving for Georgia right as we were getting ready to practice for our trip to Hawaii. That day was interesting in that, in our meeting we didn't even talk about the game we were going to play or the team or anything. We talked about what was the next step as far as the program. The other coaches found out just like everybody else found out, through the press conference. Our whole meeting came down to letting the younger players know what their options might be. The older players figured they needed to get a petition together and let the athletic director know who they wanted to be the next head coach. Both the offensive and defensive coordinators were going to go after the head-coaching job. That season, 1995, was KU's second winning season in a row and the second Bowl game during my time there. It was also KU's first 10-win season in what, 90 years or so?

Jason Thoren on
Mason Taking the Georgia Job

When we found Coach Mason was leaving for Georgia, it was tough on us because of the way we felt about him. We knew that either Coach Hankwitz or Coach Ruel would probably get the job—it was one of those years where we were really close to the coaches. Overall, though, we were happy for Coach Mason, and we knew we would be in good hands after he left, too. When you have a chance to coach at a school like Georgia, you have to consider it. It's one of the premiere schools in the country. It's a credit to the hard work he's put into the profession that he had the opportunity to go there. Still, it was definitely hard on us. I'm not going to say that we were happy or even indifferent. We were not happy about it. We loved playing for the guy, and it was hard.

Headed North

After accepting the University of Georgia's head coaching position the year before—only to relinquish it a week later—Glen Mason made it stick the second time around and left Kansas to accept the job as the University of Minnesota's head football coach.

Mason created a whirlwind situation at the end of the 1995 season by accepting the Georgia job, and then backing out just hours before his Jayhawk team took the field against UCLA in the Aloha Bowl. The inspired KU players subsequently thrashed the Bruins, 51-30. There was no bowl game this season for KU, though. Mason said that he was "sorry to leave Kansas," and that he had "left a lot of blood and sweat in Kansas."

Jason Thoren. *University of Kansas Archives*

CHAPTER 11

Mark Mangino— Building a Program

"He's going to recruit big-time talent, and when they get there he's going to make them play to the best of their ability. He's not going to accept anything less. He may not be your best friend, that's not his job. His job is to win games and make you the best player you can be."

—Harrison Hill, on Coach Mark Mangino

Five years after Glen Mason's departure, the Kansas football program was in virtually the same condition it was in 1987—the Jayhawks were horrible. Mason's successor, Terry Allen, had won just 20 games in that time period, and was dismissed before the end of the 2001 season. Once again Kansas needed someone to right its sinking football fortunes, and once again it appeared the right man for the job was selected.

When Mark Mangino was named the 35th head coach in the history of KU's football program, he knew a difficult task was at hand. He came to Kansas from Oklahoma, where he had served as the Sooners' assistant head coach/offensive coordinator for three years.

"The kids didn't feel good about themselves," Mangino said reflecting on his first days at KU. "Nobody had anything good to say about KU football. The kids were depressed and down. I knew that I had to do something pretty quickly to build them up, or we would never get this thing off the ground."

The Jayhawks finished 2-10 his first season at the helm—including an 0-8 record in the Big 12—but were the surprise team of the conference in 2003, finishing 6-6 in the regular season. A bid to the Tangerine Bowl topped off the successful campaign.

"We have got a long way to go, but we are moving in the right direction," Mangino said, "and that is all I care about as a coach."

Mark Mangino's Statement on Turning Around KU's Football Program

You have to start number one by the attitude, setting the tempo, the attitude of your program. The way we plan on doing that is coming in here and these players who are already at the University of Kansas are the University of Kansas's players and that makes them my players. We're going to get to work with the kids that we have right here and make them work hard and believe in the things that we're trying to do. The only way that we can do that is if we spell everything out about what our expectations are and what direction we want to go in. We have to, from this point, do a really good job evaluating

The Jayhawks and Tigers played before a packed Memorial Stadium in the 2003 renewal of the Border War. Kansas won, 35-14. *Photo by Jeff Jacobsen*

and recruiting good personnel. I wouldn't be sitting here today if I didn't believe that we could get this thing going in the right direction and be successful here. ...These are uncharted waters for me, but I've been very fortunate to work for two of the best football coaches in America in Bill Snyder and Bob Stoops. The only thing that I can tell you is that I took good notes in the meetings.

Don Fambrough on Mangino's Program

You know, I'm 81 years old and I go to practice every day. Coach Mangino makes me feel like I'm one of the members of the program. He makes me feel like I'm important, whether I am or not. It's just a tremendous feeling that someone who loves football and loves KU as much as I do has that kind of opportunity. You know he doesn't let just anybody else come out there and watch practice. I'm out there every day, and he's just been super to me. He's made an old coach feel like he was still part of the team.

Mark Mangino on
Building Success at KU

Winning puts people in the seats. When I first arrived here, people told me about the marketing campaigns. I think they are great because they bring out an awareness about football. Winning is the only thing that fills the stadium. We are finding some success early. We have always had a loyal core of fans, and now that fan base is expanding. Our student body is extremely excited and has great enthusiasm. What it boils down to is, if you put a good product on the field and you win, then people will come and support it. It creates a big-time college atmosphere that every program strives to have.

In the early stages I want to be able to play some teams at home so we have an opportunity to build confidence in the program. I don't know what the future holds, but 10-12 years from now, I don't want to play all of the non-conference games at home against teams we can beat. I think in five or six years if you can get your program on its feet, then you go out and play some top 25 teams from time to time. I think an example of that is Oklahoma. They came off the national championship, and they could have played a lot of teams that would be easy game, but they went out and played Alabama and UCLA. If you want to be among the best programs in the country, then you have to tangle with top-25 teams in non-conference play. We are not ready for that yet.

I see that the chemistry of our ball club is starting to develop. This is a close-knit group of kids and they worked really hard in the off season. We held the players to higher standards in the off season and they were able to bond. The process started with the winter workouts into the spring and then in the summer workouts. At two-a-days, I really saw this group come together. They are a bunch of kids who believe in each other and believe in themselves. They have a high level of confidence, and this is a group of kids that will not collapse in the face of adversity. They are going to keep going, and that's the mark of a good football team. I think that you always have a chance when you have good team chemistry and team unity.

Harrison Hill

I think Coach Mangino had perfect timing because his strengths were the exact weaknesses that we had. His biggest strength was that he was an extremely hard-nosed, tough disciplinarian. That was something we were lacking. Number two, I think Coach Mangino is a better recruiter. He recruited me when he was at K-State when I was in high school. I felt nothing for K-State, and he almost got me there because he was so charismatic and caring. He made me love K-State when there was nothing to love about it. I think those are the two things that are going to change the program. He's going to recruit big-time talent, and when they get there he's going to make them play to the best of their ability. He's not going to accept anything less. He may not be your best friend, that's not his job. His job is to win games and make you the best player you can be. That's what Coach Mangino is going to do. First day he stood up in conditioning, you knew it was a different regime. He was calling out players who weren't giving their all and chewing them out. He brought in the hammer, and it was a different mindset from day one. KU football had changed as soon as he got there, and it was a welcome change for most of us.

Mark Mangino on Accepting the 2003 Tangerine Bowl Invitation

We are very appreciative of the fact the Mazda Tangerine Bowl invited us to participate in their bowl game. We are looking forward to it. Our players are very excited and looking forward to playing in the Tangerine Bowl against North Carolina State—a very fine team. We have been practicing and recruiting and doing the kinds of things bowl teams do at this time of the year. Our kids have a bounce in their step on the practice field because it has been such a long time since they have had an opportunity to participate in a bowl here at Kansas. I am really happy for our players. . . It is an exciting time here in the KU football office because our young men have earned the opportunity to play in a bowl game.

Bill Whittemore on Mark Mangino

Before a game, Coach Mangino just kind of walks around, doesn't say much. He'd always come up to me and tell me to relax or go out there and have fun. My senior year he was a lot calmer, with me anyway. My junior year coming in, he was very intense. Every time I came off the field he'd tell me how he felt and what he'd want me to do. My senior year he kind of gave me a little more room. He let me do my own thing as far as mental prepa-

Mark Mangino receives a Gatorade bath following KU's win over Iowa State in 2003 that virtually locked up a Tangerine Bowl bid. *Photo by Jeff Jacobsen*

ration and the other stuff. He was awesome my senior year. He wanted us to go out there and have fun. He knew we were going to play our hardest. He knew that we were prepared. He knew that he had prepared us well and it was payday.

Mark Mangino on Bill Whittemore

Nobody really wanted Bill. He had his arm in a sling after having surgery on his throwing arm. Not many people were recruiting him. I saw this guy at Fort Scott making all these plays against Garden City. He was throwing the ball, he was pulling it down and running and he was flipping to people downfield. When I called they told me he was a heck of a player but he had surgery on his throwing shoulder. He came up and he liked it, and he ended up being the player we thought he could be.

(Against Missouri in 2003) his poise and management of the game were outstanding. He made plays where he needed to. When we called his number to be the ball carrier he made some people miss and got extra yards. He got into the right checks at the line of scrimmage. He threw the ball extremely well. The kids fed off him and they could see his poise and confidence.

CHAPTER 12

Gameday on the Hill

"Perhaps the finest expression of youth lies in intercollegiate athletics, where men ungrudgingly give their best and sometimes more than that not merely for love of combat but also for love of school."

—The 1931 Jayhawker Yearbook

Playing football at the University of Kansas transcends winning and losing. Won-loss records seem to mean less to the players and coaches as the years pass—individual growth and meaningful relationships are the things that endure.

"What I got from KU—I don't care what the environment is, I don't care what the circumstance is—you stay focused, you achieve, you accomplish and you come out a winner," Curtis McClinton said of his time at Kansas. "KU made that impression on me. Hopefully, one day I'll be able to pay that back to the university."

The student-athletes and coaches who have been a part of the KU football program ultimately place the overall experience of doing battle at Memorial Stadium on a different playing field in a different game—the game of life. Making the best of bad situations—as well as the best of the best—and making them even better.

Kelly Donohoe

I still draw on a daily basis as a coach what I experienced in picking myself up and going forward at KU. I look back on that experience, and maybe I put too much pressure on myself, but every day was a battle. For four years, it was a battle to keep my starting quarterback job, and I never felt there was a time when I could sit back and enjoy it because I was always fighting like heck to keep my position, and I was fighting like heck with the others just to establish KU as a decent program. I think those experiences I'll always use, and I always will when things are tough in life. And even today if my team loses a game—and we've been successful—I get them to bounce back. That's why I think that athletics at any level is critical to people's lives because of what you learn. You hear it all the time: sacrifice, dedication and teamwork. But, that's what life is when you get older. When you own a company or are part of a company, when you have those moments, those pressure times, you're going to help your company a little bit better. That's what I take out of my experience more than anything, other than the tremendous relationships I formed with teammates and the coaches.

Here I am, 15 years later, and I'm going up to the Minnesota football clinic due to the fact that I still have a good relationship with Coach Mason and Coach Brown and some of the other coaches. I think that's special that after all those years I still stay in touch with the people who meant something to me. What Coach Mason did for me in my life was incredible, because he took a guy who was coming off a horrible sophomore season at quarterback and believed in me. I will never forget when he pulled me aside one afternoon after a workout down in that hallway of the old football area that we had and he said, "I've coached quarterbacks who have had hard seasons, but you are the toughest quarterback that I've been around." I don't know if he 100 percent meant that, but I do think that was his way of making me believe in myself. I remember what that meant to me, the confidence he gave me in myself. By being a starter those last two years at KU, what that's done for me in my career professionally, all the credibility it's given me—I owe him so much for that, and also to Dave Warner, who was the quarterback coach. It would have been very easy my after sophomore year to say, "I'm not a player at this level, I need to go do something else." Because that's how bad it was.

I will always appreciate what Coach Mason did for me to give me that confidence. I think he felt sorry for me because he saw how much the opposing teams beat the hell out of me. I took an ass whooping every Saturday. To just bounce back, I think he appreciated that. I know he liked guys like that. His big thing was to tell us that "You're all a bunch of tough suckers." I kind of take that tone with my players today.

Nolan Cromwell

It was a great experience playing for Kansas, and I have great memories of KU. I think it really helped established me as an athlete, number one, because they let me run track and play football. The opportunity to really show my athletic ability is probably why I was drafted where I was drafted by the NFL. I can still remember my mom and dad, getting up at 4 a.m., driving from western Kansas to KU, having a tailgate before the game, then coming to see me afterwards. Then they would drive all the way back home. They lived for Saturdays to come and watch the football game. To be part of something that was really exciting.

For a little farm boy from Kansas to line up at a major college football level and compete and play, I just thank KU for giving me the opportunity. The school really took a chance on me being from a small town in western Kansas. I played 1A football in high school, and to offer a full-ride scholarship to me without knowing if I could play with bigger kids was maybe a gamble on their part. And they didn't know if I could learn the complexity of the offense and defense. They took a chance on me, and I think it worked out for them, and it worked for me.

Bobby Douglas

To me, playing at Kansas was a great experience, especially because we were able to have a football team that got better and better, and I was a pretty big part of that. I was able to succeed at a school that I still love. I had some of my greatest times, not just playing football, but at the University. I know tons of people who have gone there, that I went to school with, and who have gone there since—I have a real affection for the University of Kansas. So it's really the great experience I had being able to play football and go to school there, meeting all the friends that I have had for a lifetime. Kansas is a great school, and it's a great place to go to school. All those things were so positive, it was a great experience and I'll never forget it.

Marlin Blakeney

Although we're not known for strong traditions, and KU is primarily a basketball school, I think the years I played football we showed that we had a great team. I think that all the guys in my class who started also graduated together. Everyone talks about Coach Mason. He had the respect of the team. Being a Jayhawk is awesome, and following the Jayhawks, whether it be football, basketball or whatever, everywhere I go I run into Jayhawks from coast to coast. It's good to be part of the family, and part of the school's athletic history.

Bobby Skahan

Playing football at KU is probably in the top three experiences of my life—the contact and the association of the people both in and outside of sports. It was just a great school to play for. The alumni and the people I've been associated with since I was there have been a great thing for me. Most of my closest friends are from that association. Jim Ryun and I became very good friends. The reason we were good friends was that after I was hurt, I had to go the hospital. He and I drove over together. I couldn't walk, so he pushed me around in a wheelchair in the medical center—we couldn't find where we were going. I'm friends with many of the guys I played with, like Gale and so many others. All I have are good memories.

Bert Coan

I liked the atmosphere of KU's campus, it was a real college atmosphere—I don't know how to put it exactly. If you go to some schools, it's like being downtown at rush hour. It seemed liked KU had the perfect setting and everything, it was just a great college town. I enjoyed my years there a lot, spending time with my teammates and what have you. I played with a great bunch of guys. But looking back at KU, I guess the campus setting, how beautiful it was, is the one thing I liked more than anything else.

Jason Thoren

I think the thing that was really great at KU and playing football at KU was the 11 guys in the huddle. Eleven guys with completely different mental make-ups who got together and performed as one. There were a lot of times that huddle was like a party. I mean we really had fun playing. You'd turn and look at Dick Holt who had had four surgeries and was probably never going to play again, and you're holding his hand. To me that was just inspirational.

I think in the years that I played we were able to accomplish a lot. It meant a great deal to me after growing up and watching some of the hardships the program went

Bert Coan. *University of Kansas Archives*

through. Some of the older people who were around Lawrence, Kansas City, or Topeka when KU was a good football team, they hadn't seen a good team in some time. It meant a great deal to me to see those older guys smile again and come back around and cheer us on. Growing up in Lawrence, it was very special for me to see KU win again. To be out there on the field, playing in a Kansas uniform, was just an incredible dream come true.

Don Fambrough

I think every coach I've been around has a burning desire that someday he can coach his alma mater. And to be a head football coach to me—I love the game so much, I love coaching so much—to have the opportunity to be a head coach, I can't think of the words that would describe the feeling. But if you want to double that feeling, then be a head coach at the school where you played football, where you have roots. I've been blessed, I've been so lucky. I think that every coach who ever had the opportunity to coach at his alma mater has the same feelings that I do.

Emmett Edwards

It means a great deal to me to have played football at KU. I hold that experience in high esteem. Going to Kansas was great—I couldn't have asked for anything better. A great environment existed to play ball, and also to obtain a degree. Plus, I was very fortunate to be around some outstanding coaches, teammates and alumni who adhered to the university and held it in high esteem. Kansas is a great place to go, and a great place to be from.

John Hadl

Growing up, that's what I wanted to do—play football for Kansas. When I was in grade school, I would walk up to practice every day and watch the team. I knew every player on the team, and I'd sneak into every game with a couple guys in town. We didn't miss anything, football, basketball, we saw it all. Every single time KU was at home I would be at the game, and in those days it was always a lot of fun. I can remember sneaking in and actually getting down on the sidelines and standing next to Oklahoma coach Bud Wilkinson during a game when I was in seventh grade or so. I was just standing there, and he looked down at me, walked on by and didn't say a word.

Max Ediger

Back then, football was really everything. It was my life. It was definitely a lot of fun, and I don't know about the other players, but I really enjoyed the practices, the camaraderie. Being associated with a lot of top athletes from around the country was great. Back then they had a training table, and we'd go down there and get three buffets for breakfast, lunch and dinner. Being around those types of athletes and sitting around the training table—they've got pictures of Wilt Chamberlain and Gayle Sayers, John Riggins, displayed on the tables. All these players you hear about are some of the top athletes who have ever participated in athletics at KU. I think at the time when we were playing at KU, we were third in the country with active NFL players.

I have good feelings about it when I look back and think about all the times. It just goes so quick, so fast. You

Max Ediger had a 71-yard touchdown run against K-State in 1977. *University of Kansas Archives*

just don't realize at the time how much you fun you had until it's all over. Every good athlete, regardless of what he plays, comes to the realization that at some point you've got to hang up your cleats. As far as the university goes, we had strong backing, great alumni. It was a great atmosphere to play in. What an awesome campus with the shade on the hill from all those trees—there's a lot of tradition there.

Pepper Rodgers

Coaching at Kansas was like my first baby or my first love. It was just very special. We had a group of young coaches who went on later to be very successful themselves. We had a wonderful senior coach (Don Fambrough) who went on to be the coach of Kansas twice, who I'm crazy about as a person and a coach. I remember the famous relay race that we had fun doing—before the season started we divided the offensive players up against the defense and ran a five-mile relay inside Allen Fieldhouse. That was fun. We always did things that were fun. It was my first head coaching job, we were successful and we went to the Orange Bowl. I consider Kansas to be a very important part of my life.

L.T. Levine

It meant a great deal to me to have played at KU. I think I learned a lot in my time there. Not only in Lawrence, but in the state of Kansas and playing football. To some people that's their life. It's amazing what kind of an influence you are on them. It's just a great feeling to know that you're playing for someone and something. Those people believe in you. To do something for them and give back all you can is great, and it's great to be a part of that family. I feel like it is a family because it's a small school and a small town. A lot of people could have gone somewhere else, but they still took their chances to go to a school that doesn't get as much publicity. If I had to do it all over again, I would still go to Kansas.

Curtis McClinton

If you look up the 1961 team that went to the Bluebonnet Bowl, I was the only black player. There were other emerging players, and of course, right after me came the great, great Gale Sayers. Even during his era, he marched on campus for integration and better times. That's what KU did for me and for a lot of other individuals that were of my race. We became individuals who are able to deal with that in a flex type of way and deal with what is important. If we didn't study, we would have been kicked out of KU and it didn't make any difference about ethnicity. So you learn to deal with your priorities. It's the same thing with football. You learn to play the game to win. So what I got from KU—I don't care what the environment is, I don't care what the circumstance is— you stay focused, you achieve, you accomplish and you come out a winner. KU made that impression on me. Hopefully, one day I'll be able to pay that back to the university.

Otto Schnellbacher

I was thrilled to death that I could play for KU. I was really pleased to be part of KU's 1946-47 teams. I wasn't too happy in 1942 because football wasn't that important to the coaching staff and the players. When you get into a situation where you have teammates who want and need to be successful, it's a very exciting time. If you know Don Fambrough, you know he vibrates excitement. Ray Evans did, too. You had people who, when you got into a crucial part of the game, you could trust. You knew they were going to give you everything they had, they weren't going to walk away on you. It was an exciting time. My 1942-43 basketball team was the same way. We would have won the NCAA if we hadn't gone in the service. There's something about the makeup of the team that jelled and fit. Same thing with the 1947 football team. We had a ball club that jelled. We had people who could excel at things. You didn't have anybody quitting or backing off. There was none of this giving-up type of attitude. I really enjoyed the people I played with. We've been able to have a reunion every five years since the Orange Bowl. When the guys walk into the room, the same esprit de corps, the same love, the same feeling, the same respect that I had for them back then is still there. And that included the guys who didn't play very much. Everybody had respect for everybody else. It was a great family, and they continue to be a family to this day.

Mike Hubach

I'm very proud that I was given the opportunity to play and be a part of KU's tradition, the tradition that it has in all sports. The people involved there were just fantastic—from the athletic department to the citizens of Lawrence, Kansas, to the people around the country who are as proud of the university as I am. I just wish I would have known what I wanted to do with myself at the time I went to school. I wish I would have had an idea of what to major in.

Chip Budde

It was loads and loads of fun playing football at KU. I would say it was a defining experience in my life and I hope it was the same for the guys I played with. Playing in the Blue-Gray All-Star game, I met guys who went through the same things at different universities, and I'm sure they developed the sort of friendships I did. You know we didn't win a lot of games, and I think that made us closer as a team. And I wouldn't trade any of my teammates for a single victory, because I love the guys I played with. Playing football for KU was a very special thing for me, even though we didn't do as well as we had hoped. I got a good education and I met a great bunch of people, that's really what it comes down to.

Spencer Bonner

It actually means a great deal to me to have played football at KU. The friends that I made, and the school itself being a top-notch educational system are both special. Then, to be part of the program during the time I was a part of it is something I'm always going to remember, and something that I'm going to be proud of regardless of my playing time. I can always say that I was part of KU during a very good time—from 1991-1995 we only had one losing season, went to two bowl games and had a 10 and 2 record on my way out. I may not have played as a starter at my position, but everything else the team wanted me to do, I was able to do. I'm always going to have a lot of loyalty toward KU. I'm quite happy about Mark Mangino becoming the head coach and the things he's already achieved at Kansas.

Ray Evans

Growing up in Kansas City and Dad having been at KU, it really was a childhood dream of mine—I really, really wanted to play football for KU. Having Coach Fambrough to make it such a great experience was a blast. It was beyond what I might have hoped for, other than getting hurt. That was the only disappointing thing. The friends I made were just tremendous. I can't imagine it other than not getting hurt and having a few more bowl games in the mix. It was an awesome experience, it really was.

Mike Norseth

I feel like I played at the highest level there is in college football. I played at a school that is a great place to go to college. I can still remember my first game against Wichita State. We took the bus from the Holidome over to the stadium with the police escort and all the fans and the band coming down the hill. To be there, and to be the starting quarterback at the highest level of college football is an outstanding feeling. And my parents were there—they went to every game during my two years at KU, and were very proud. I think KU was very special to them as well. After all the things you put on your parents through growing up, its great to give back to them. Most people don't realize I played in the NFL, but they are usually in awe when I tell them I started for two years at Kansas.

From a football perspective, I wished it would be more of a football school than a basketball school. I don't think that's going to change anytime soon, unfortunately. We also had a lot of academic issues my senior year. If we could have had everyone eligible who was supposed to be eligible, I think we could have been a 9-3 or 10-2 team very easily. As far as the atmosphere and the college, I am proud to say that I am from Kansas. In fact my nickname in the NFL was "Jayhawk."

Charlie Hoag

I went to Oklahoma and I met Jack Mitchell when he was still at Oklahoma and I was totally impressed. And I was really going to go—well, I thought I was going to go to Oklahoma—and I told my folks. They were so upset because they wanted me to go to Kansas. They wouldn't express it until I wanted to go to Oklahoma and they were so upset. I went to bed that night and had trouble sleeping because they were so upset. I got up the next morning and told them I was going to Kansas and the press got hold of it and it was in the newspaper and that was it. And I'm glad I did. Football-wise, I probably would have been better off at Oklahoma, but overall, basketball and everything, being able to go to the Olympics and playing on the National Championship basketball team, it was much better for me at KU. But I love football. You know to be quite honest, thinking about everything, I really loved football on Saturday afternoons with the bright, brisk sun—it was quite a thrill.

Chip Hilleary

To go from not knowing anything about Kansas football to now, I can sum it up by saying that I bleed crimson and blue—once a Jayhawk always a Jayhawk. My kids know the Jayhawk fight song now. We are very loyal supporters of the football program. When I watch the team play today, I get just as excited as the first time I got to play for Kansas. I know that there will be a day when the tradition will continue. I think what is being done now with the program reflects what Coach Mason went through. When I think of Kansas football, I think of people like Tony Sands. I think of Kelly Donohoe, a good guy. He's done very well. When I think of Kansas football, I think of the hard work just to gain respect. Being such a basketball school and overshadowed by that, it takes a lot of hard work to make the football program shine. Every time I watch a football game it brings back the good memories I had at Kansas. Saturday afternoons, there's nothing like riding the bus from Kansas City to Lawrence on K-10 and having that feeling you get with the camaraderie in the locker room. After the game, win or lose, you have the loyal KU fans to support you. Those are the kinds of things that I will always remember. I'm blessed that I even had an opportunity to be a part of the Kansas football program. I had a great time in Lawrence.

Harrison Hill

It makes me feel proud to have played football at KU. No matter what my record was, no matter how many bowl games we didn't go to, no matter how many times we struggled, I was proud to put on a jersey that said "Kansas." When I walked out that tunnel, I felt proud because I knew about all the great players who had played before me, and I knew I was playing for them. I knew I was playing for John Hadl and Gale Sayers. I knew that Nolan Cromwell had played before me and I knew how much it meant to them. I felt honored wearing the jersey and playing out there. I wouldn't take anything back no matter how many games we lost. I wouldn't change it—I would have still gone to KU. I loved my experience and it was a great university. I think it has so much potential to become a great football powerhouse with Mangino and the new system. People want to come to KU. Recruits wanted to come to a school like KU with a beautiful campus, great academics and a cool town. It's as fun for me now to sit back and watch games or to read articles in the Lawrence newspaper. Now I'm anxious to see how great we're going to become.

Kerwin Bell

I made some very great friends at KU, that's the most important thing. I come back to KU, and football is football. Sure, I could have done some things differently when I was there, or I could have gone somewhere else, and who knows what would have happened? The most important thing is that when I come back to Lawrence, I'm welcomed, and that's a good, heartwarming feeling no matter where I'm at in town. The basketball connections I have—that's the first thing I did my first spring break at KU, Frank Seurer and I went to Wichita for the NCAA tournament. We did that every spring break. So, I've got a lot of basketball friends. And I knew Coach Self. He was first there in 1985, that's when I came back to school. I played basketball with him on our lunch break. I sat in his living room back in 1998 when he was at Tulsa breaking down game film after they played Fresno State. Danny Manning and I had a softball team together. I'm just fortunate enough to have a relationship with the school, and that comes from me and Frank Seurer sticking it out, graduating from KU, especially after we came in with a lot of fanfare.

Kerwin Bell. *KUAC Media Relations*

Bill Whittemore

Kansas saved me. They were the only Division I school that wanted me. They gave me the chance to showcase my talents, to play against the best and to see if I could really play at that level. I really have to thank Coach Mangino for giving me that opportunity.

Kansas is an awesome university. It represents everything I believe in, it's got great people associated with the program—it's just a great school. It's almost like, as a Tennessee boy finding Kansas, something drove me there for a reason and I'm very thankful that I ended up at KU. I was always treated properly and fairly. The thing I'm most grateful for is this: you can go to school at your Notre Dames, Ohio States, Alabamas—the historical programs—but what was so awesome about Kansas is that unlike those schools, we didn't have the show dogs, guys on the team who wouldn't have anything to do with their teammates. Kansas was different—all the guys got along great. It didn't matter who or what you were. And that's what I'm going to miss the most, hanging out with the guys and just having a good time, messing around. That's what made Kansas so special, and that's what I'll miss most, the group of guys we had. KU draws goodhearted, willing athletes, and I'm very glad I landed there.

Celebrate the Heroes of Kansas Sports
in These Other Releases from Sports Publishing!

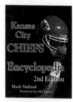

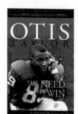
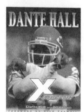

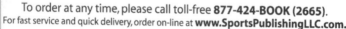